Aboriginal American Authors

by

Daniel G. Brinton

Aboriginal American Authors
by Daniel G. Brinton

ISBN: 978-93-59954-61-5

Published by

DOUBLE 9 BOOKS

2/13-B, Ansari Road
Daryaganj, New Delhi – 110002
info@double9books.com
www.double9books.com
Tel. 011-40042856

ABOUT THE AUTHOR

Daniel Garrison Brinton (May 13, 1837 – July 31, 1899) was a surgeon, historian, archaeologist, and ethnologist from the United States. Brinton was born in Chester County, Pennsylvania, in Thornbury Township. Brinton graduated from Yale University in 1858 and spent the next year traveling in Europe after attending Jefferson Medical College for two years. He pursued his studies further in Paris and Heidelberg. During the American Civil War, he served as a surgeon in the Union army from 1862 to 1865, serving as surgeon-in-charge of the US Army general hospital in Quincy, Illinois, from 1864 to 1865. Brinton got sunburned at Missionary Ridge (the Third Battle of Chattanooga) and was never able to travel in extremely hot weather again. This handicap has an impact on his work as an ethnologist.

CONTENTS

NEW INTRODUCTION

Aboriginal American Authors, published by the Anthropologist Daniel G. Brinton in 1883, is a work that is particularly appropriate for our own times. The native American movement has stressed the need for history written from the Indian point of view. Interest in native American literature has become an important component in reinforcing a sense of identity among American Indians today.

Brinton's work is a good summary of the better known traditional writings of Indians from many regions of the Western hemisphere. This bibliographical survey provides information on tribal histories that would be particularly useful for Indian Study Programs in the states of Oklahoma, New York and Wisconsin.

Brinton was aware of the 19th century racism of many who wrote about the American Indian and reacted against it in his writings by taking a stance which in some ways anticipates Ruth Benedict's involvement in similar questions half a century later. Aboriginal American Authors is written as an early attempt at placing the literature of the American Indian with the other great literary traditions of the world; that is why its usefulness endures.

John Hobgood
Social Science Department
Chicago State College
1970

PREFACE

The present memoir is an enlargement of a paper which I laid before the *Congres International des Americanistes*, when acting as a delegate to its recent session in Copenhagen, August, 1883. The changes are material, the whole of the text having been re-written and the notes added.

It does not pretend to be an exhaustive bibliographical essay, but was designed merely to point out to an intelligent and sympathetic audience a number of relics of Aboriginal American Literature, and to bespeak the aid and influence of that learned body in the preservation and publication of these rare documents.

Philadelphia, Nov. 1883.

Section 1.
Introductory

When even a quite intelligent person hears about "Aboriginal American Literature," he is very excusable for asking: What is meant by the term? Where is this literature? In fine, Is there any such thing?

To answer such inquiries, I propose to treat, with as much brevity as practicable, of the literary efforts of the aborigines of this continent, a chapter in the general History of Literature hitherto wholly neglected.

Indeed, it will be a surprise to many to learn that any members of these rude tribes have manifested either taste or talent for scholarly productions. All alike have been regarded as savages, capable, at best, of but the most limited culture.

Such an opinion has been fostered by prejudices of race, by the jealousy of castes, and in our own day by preconceived theories of evolution. That it is erroneous, can, I think, be easily shown.

Let us first inquire into the existence of

Section 2.
The Literary Faculty in the Native Mind

This faculty is indicated by a vivid imagination, a love of narration, and an ample, appropriate, and logically developed vocabulary. That, as a race, the aborigines of America possessed these qualifications to a remarkable degree, is attested by many witnesses who have lived intimately among them; and is only denied by those whose acquaintance with them has been superficial, or derived from second-hand and doubtful sources.

The red man peoples air, earth, and the waters with countless creatures of his fancy; his expressions are figurative and metaphorical; he is quick to seize analogies; and when he cannot explain he is ever ready to invent. This is shown in his inappeasable love of story telling. As a *raconteur* he is untiring. He has, in the highest degree, Goethe's *Lust zu fabuliren*. In no Oriental city does the teller of strange tales find a more willing audience than in the Indian wigwam. The folk lore of every tribe which has been properly investigated has turned out to be most ample. Tales of talking animals, of mythical warriors, of giants, dwarfs, subtle women, potent magicians, impossible adventures, abound to an extent that defies collection.[1]

Nor are these narratives repeated in a slip-shod, negligent style. The hearers permit no such carelessness. They are sticklers for nicety of expression; for clear and well turned periods; for vivid and accurate description; for flowing and sonorous sentences. As a rule, their languages lend themselves readily to these demands. It is a singular error, due wholly to ignorance of the subject, to maintain that the American tongues are cramped in their vocabularies, or that their syntax does not permit them to define the more delicate relationships of ideas. Nor is it less a mistake to assert, as has been done repeatedly, and even by authorities of eminence in our own day, that they are not capable of supplying the expressions of abstract reasonings. Although pure abstractions were rarely objects of interest to these children of nature, many, if not most, of their tongues favor the formation of expressions which are as thoroughly transcendental as any to be found in the *Kritik der Reinen Vernunft*.[2]

Their literary faculty is further demonstrated in the copiousness of their vocabularies, their rare facility of expression, and their natural aptitude for the acquisition of other languages. Theophilie Gautier used to say, that the most profitable book for a professional writer to read is the dictionary; that is, that a mastery of words is his most valuable acquirement. The extraordinarily rich synonomy of some American tongues, notably the Algonkin, the Aztec, and the Qquichua, attests how sedulously their resources have been cultivated. Father Olmos, in his grammar of the Aztec, gives many examples of twenty and thirty synonymous expressions, all in current use in his day. A dictionary, in my possession, of the Maya, one of the least plastic of American tongues, gives over thirty thousand words, and scarcely a hundred of them of foreign extraction.

This linguistic facility is shown also in the ease with which they acquire foreign languages. "It is not uncommon," says Dr. Washington Matthews, speaking of the Hidatsa, by no means a specially brilliant tribe, "to find persons among them, some even under twenty years of age, who can speak fluently four or five different languages."[3] Mr. Stephen Powers tells us that, in California, he found many Indians speaking three, four, five or more languages, generally including English;[4] and in South America, both Humboldt and D'Orbigny express their surprise at the same fact, which they repeatedly observed.[5]

But the most tangible evidence of both their linguistic and literary ability is the work some of these natives have accomplished in European tongues. It does not come within the limits of my plan to enter fully into an examination of this branch of literature; but it is worth while mentioning some of the more prominent native writers, who have composed in European languages, as their productions are an easy test of what the faculties of the red race are in this direction.

As the colonizers of the New World have been chiefly from Spain and Great Britain, so naturally the English and Spanish languages have been brought most widely to the knowledge of the natives. The half-civilized tribes, within the area of the United States, have produced several authors of merit. Perhaps the earliest of these was David Cusick, who, in 1825, printed his *Ancient History of the Six Nations*. He was a full blood Tuscarora, and his English is far from correct. Yet the arrangement of his matter is skillful, and some passages quaintly vivid and forcible. Another member of the Iroquois confederacy, Peter Dooyentate Clarke, has taken up the *Origin and Traditional History of the Wyandotts*, and has made a readable little book (published at Toronto, 1870); while still more lately, Chief Elias Johnson, of the Tuscaroras, has published a *History of the Six Nations*, very creditably composed. (Lockport, 1881.)

The tribes of Algonkin lineage can also count some respectable writers. The Rev. William Apess (or Apes), a member of the Pequod tribe of Massachusetts, wrote and published five or six small books and pamphlets, on questions relating to his people, between 1829 and 1837. The book of George Copway, or Kah-ge-ga-gah-bowh, a chief of the Ojibways, on *The Traditional History of the Ojibway Nation* (London, 1850), is a good authority on the topic, and so well written that we can scarcely suppose that it was his unaided effort. Of almost equal merit is the *History of the Ojibway Indians, with especial reference to their Conversion to Christianity*, by the Rev. Peter Jones, or Kahkewaquonaby, a full-blood Indian, (London, 1861.)

In the southwest, the *Cherokee Phoenix* offered a medium through which the native writers of that tribe frequently published original contributions; and one of its early editors, Elias Boudinot (named after the celebrated philanthropist), published separately a number of addresses and other documents, in English.

But, as we might naturally expect, it is in Spanish that we find the best work of the native writers. The partly civilized races of Mexico, Central America and Peru, were much better prepared to receive the lessons of European teachers than the barbarous hunting tribes. Had they had any fair chance, they would have soon equaled their teachers. Father Motolinia, one of the earliest missionaries to Mexico, testifies to the readiness with which the natives acquired both Spanish and Latin, and adds that, in the latter tongue, they became skilled grammarians, and wrote both verse and prose with commendable accuracy.[6] Quite a long list of such native Latinists, their names and their writings, is given by Father Augustin de Vetancurt, and he is not sparing in his praise of the ability they displayed in the use of both Spanish and Latin.[7] Similar testimony is rendered of the natives of Guatemala, by the Archbishop Garcia Pelaez. He mentions, by name, several Indians who became conspicuously thorough Latin scholars, and refers to others who won honors in all the faculties of the University of Guatemala, and distinguished themselves in after life by the display of their talents and education.[8] Nor would it be difficult to find many other such examples in Peru and Brazil.

The list of native Mexicans who wrote in Spanish is a fairly long one; and I need only mention the better known names. At the head should be placed that of Don Fernando de Alva Ixtlilxochitl. He was a lineal descendant of the sovereigns of Tezcuco, and an ardent student of the antiquities of his race. Among the many works which he wrote are the *Relaciones Historicas* and the *Historia Chichimeca*, which were published by Lord Kingsborough; a *Historia de la Nueva Espana*, a *Historia del Reyno de Tezcuco*, and a *Historia de Nuestra Senora de Guadalupe*, which have not had the fortune to be printed.

Such an excellent critic as Mr. Prescott says of his style: "His language is simple, and occasionally eloquent and touching. His descriptions are highly picturesque. He abounds in familiar anecdote; and the natural graces of his manner in detailing the more striking events of history and the personal adventures of his heroes, entitle him to the name of the Livy of Anahuac."

Ixtlilxochitl flourished about the year 1600, and among his contemporaries was Fernando de Alvarado Tezozomoc, also of native blood, whose *Cronica Mexicana* has been preserved, and is considered to be well written, but less reliable. Of about the same date are the *Relacion* of Juan Bautista de Tomar, a native of Tezcuco, in which he treats of the customs of his ancestors; the *Relaciones* of Don Antonio Pimentel, grandson of Nezahualpilli, lord of Tezcuco, an author quoted and praised by the historian Torquemada; the *Historia de Tlaxcallan* of Diego Munoz Camargo, a noble Tlascalan mestizo, of whose style Prescott remarks that it compares not unfavorably with that of some of the missionaries themselves; and the *Relacion de los Dioses y Ritos de la Gentilidad* of Don Pedro Ponce, the cacique of Tzumpahuacan. Somewhat later, about 1625, Don Domingo de San Anton Munon Chimalpain wrote his *Historia Mexicana* and his *Historia de la Conquista*, which have been mentioned with respect by various writers.

Along with these examples of literary culture in Mexico may be named several native Peruvian writers who made use of the language of their conquerors; as Don Joan de Santa Cruz Pachacuti Yamqui, whose *Relacion de Antiguedades de Piru* is a precious document, though composed in very uncritical Spanish; as Don Luis Inca, whose *Relacion*, prepared in Spanish, seems now to be lost, but is referred to, with praise, by some of the older writers; and, above all others, Inca Garcillasso de la Vega, whose vivid and attractive style, and numerous historical writings place him easily in the first rank of Spanish historians of America.

From the above it would seem evident enough that the American aborigines were endowed, as a race, with a turn for literary composition, and a faculty for it. They were generally, however, an unlettered race. What they composed was for oral use only. This might be carefully arranged, committed to heart, and handed down from generation to generation; but as for recording it in forms which would convey it to the mind through the eye, that was a discovery they had but partially made.

I say, "partially," because graphic methods, of some kind, were widely used. We may as well omit from consideration, in this connection, the merely pictographic signs of the hunting tribes, although they were used for mnemonic purposes. Let us rather proceed, at once, to the highest specimens of the graphic art in ancient America, and inquire their scope. In Mexico, in

Yucatan, in Nicaragua, and in one or two districts of South America, the early explorers found systems of writing which seemed to resemble that to which they were accustomed.

The Aztecs manufactured, in large quantities, a useful paper from the leaves of the maguey, and upon it they painted numerous figures and signs, which conveyed ideas, and sometimes also sounds. An early authority informs us that their books were of five kinds. The first detailed their method of computing time; the second described their holy days, festivals and religious epochs; the third gave the interpretation of dreams, omens and signs; the fourth supplied directions for naming children; and the fifth rehearsed the rites and ceremonies connected with matrimony.[9] Besides these, we know they wrote out tribute rolls, the ancient history of their tribes, the fables of their mythology, the genealogy of their sovereigns, and the geographical descriptions of territories. Of all these we have examples preserved, and many of them have been published.

Quite another and a more perfect method of writing prevailed among the Mayas of Yucatan and Central America. Their books were exceedingly neat, and strongly resembled an ordinary quarto volume, such as appears on European bookshelves. I have so lately discussed their manufacture, and the so-called alphabet in which they were written, and in a work of such easy access, that it is enough if I quote the conclusions there arrived at.[10] They are:—

1. The Maya graphic system was recognized, from the first, to be distinct from the Mexican.

2. It was a hieroglyphic system, known only to the priests and a few nobles.

3. It was employed for a variety of purposes, prominent among which was the preservation of their history and calendar.

4. It was a composite system, containing pictures (figuras), ideograms (caracteres), and phonetic signs (letras).

The ruins of Palenque, Copan, and other Maya cities, abound in such hieroglyphs.

The natives of Nicaragua, those, at least, of Aztec lineage, made use of parchment volumes, folded into a neat and portable compass, in which they painted, in red and black ink, certain figures, "by means of which," says the chronicler Oviedo, "they could express and understand whatever they wished, with entire clearness."[11]

In South America the Peruvians had their *quipus*, cords of different lengths, sizes and colors, knotted in various ways, and attached to a base cord, an arrangement that was a decided aid to the memory, though it could not be connected with the sounds of words. There are also faint traces of figures, with definite meaning, among the Muyscas of Colombia; and the Moxos of Western Bolivia are said to have employed, as late as the last century, a method of writing, consisting of lines traced on wooden slabs.[12]

Section 3.
Narrative Literature

Of all forms of sustained discourse, we may reasonably suppose that of narration to have been the earliest. The incidents of the hunt were related at the return; the experiences of the past were told as a guide to the present; and the first efforts of the imagination are the depicting of fictitious occurrences, tradition and myth, story and history; these make up most of the entertainment of conversation to simple minds.

Hence, in this primitive literature which I am describing, the narrative portion is the most abundant. There was a natural aspiration on the part of the natives, as soon as they had learned the art of writing, to preserve in permanent form the records, more or less authentic, of their tribes and ancestors. This desire of preserving the national history is shown by the works of Copway, Jones, Cusick, Ixtlilxochitl, and others, to whom I have already referred, who wrote in European tongues.

If we begin our survey at the extreme north, we find the Eskimo, amid his depressing surroundings of eternal frost and months-long nights, an unwearied chatterbox, reciting his own and his ancestors' adventures, and weaving from his fancy the most extraordinary web of fictitious experiences. Once taught to write, hundreds of these tales were committed to paper by native hands. The manuscript collection of such in the possession of the learned and indefatigable Dr. Heinrich Rink contains considerably over two thousand pages, and the charming rendering into English, which has been published by his efforts, is a storehouse of weird conceptions and partly historic traditions about the past of Greenland and Labrador. What adds to their interest is that most of the illustrations are wood-cuts by native artists, truthfully setting forth their own mental pictures.[13]

Another Eskimo composition, in the dialogue style, is before me as I write. It is the description by Pok, a Greenlander, of his journey to Europe and his return. The narrative forms a pamphlet of eighteen pages, with several quaint colored illustrations, and it is one of the rare products of the Godthaab press in Greenland to which we can assign a genuine native origin.[14]

Another, which reveals still more distinctly the artistic and imaginative capacities of that strange race, was published at Godthaab, in 1860. Mr. Field remarks of it:—"An Esquimau of Greenland, with his pencil, has, in this work, attempted to give representations of the traditions, manners, weapons and habits of life of his own race."[15]

Among the tribes of the eastern United States there were a few individuals who attempted to compose somewhat extensive records in their native languages.

One of the most curious examples is that known as the *Walum Olum*, a short account of the early history of the Delaware tribe, written in that idiom, with mnemonic symbols attached. Its history is not very complete. A "Dr. Ward, of Indiana" is said to have obtained it from a member of the nation, in 1822. From him it passed into the hands of Prof. C.S. Rafinesque, an eccentric and visionary Frenchman, who passed the later years of his life in Philadelphia. He undertook to translate it, and after his death the translation, together with the original, came into the possession of Mr. E.G. Squier. By him it was first published, but in a partial and incomplete manner, much of the original text and many of the mnemonic symbols being omitted, and no effort being made to improve Rafinesque's translation.[16]

The *Book of Rites*[17] of the Iroquois or Six Nations, lately edited by Mr. Horatio Hale, is one of the most remarkable native productions north of Mexico. Its authenticity and antiquity are indisputable. The rites it describes are the ceremonies and set speeches, the chants and formulas, of what is called "The Council of Condolence," whose function is to express the national sense of loss at the death of a chief, and to conduct the inauguration of his successor. The publication of this ritual, supported as it is with the learned notes of Mr. Hale, and an introduction by him, on the history, formation and purpose of the famous League of the Iroquois, has thrown a remarkable light, not merely on the ethnology of the district where the Iroquois were located, but on the mental characteristics of the red race in general. It is a refutation of the unscientific assumptions of a good many would-be scientific men, who are self-blinded by their theories of development to obvious facts in the mental powers of uncultivated tribes.

Of less general importance, but admirable also for competent editorship, is the short narrative of the Nipissing Chief, Francois Kaondinoketc, which was published a few years ago, both in the original and with a French translation, by a Canadian missionary, eminent alike for his piety and his learning. It recites the journey of a half-breed Christian Indian into the country of the heathen tribe of Beaver Indians, and the miraculous interposition by which his life was saved when these Pagans had caught him. They told him he must kill an eagle flying far above them; at his prayer, the bird descended and came within the reach of his sabre. In turn, he asked them to shoot their arrows into a tree; but by rubbing it with holy water, the bark was so hardened that not one of their shafts could pierce it. So they confessed the greatness of the Christian's God.[18]

This charmingly naive narrative makes us doubly regret that the editor's projected *Chrestomathie Algonquine* has not been carried out in full.

The southern Atlantic coast of the United States was principally occupied by the Muskokee or Creek tribe, who occupied the territory as far west as the Mississippi. Their language was first reduced to writing in the Greek alphabet, by the Moravian missionaries, about 1733; but at present a modified form of the English alphabet is in use. They had a very definite and curious tribal history, full of strange metaphors and obscure references. It was, according to old authorities, "written in red and black characters, on the skin of a young buffalo," and was read off from this symbolic script by their head-chief, Chekilli, to the English, in 1735, and skin and translation were both sent to London, and both lost there. But, luckily, the Moravian missionaries preserved a faithful translation of it, and this, some years ago, I brought to the notice of students of these matters.[19]

Its authenticity is beyond question, and to this day the chiefs of the Creeks recollect many of the points it contains, and have repeated it to the eminent linguist, Mr. A.S. Gatschet, who has taken it down afresh from their lips, and is preparing it for publication. Collateral evidence is also furnished by "General" Milfort, a French adventurer, who lived among the Creeks several years, toward the close of the last century, and testifies that they preserved, "by beads and belts," the memory of the adventures of their ancestors, and recited to him a long account of them, which he repeats with that negligence which everywhere marks his carelessly prepared volume. [20]

Their northern neighbors, the Cherokees, use an alphabet invented by Sequoyah, one of themselves, in 1824. It is syllabic, of eighty-five characters, and is used for printing. Sequoyah had no intention of aiding the missionaries; he preferred the "old religion," and when he saw the New Testament printed in his characters, he expressed regret that he had ever invented them. What he wanted was to teach his people useful arts, and to preserve the national traditions. I have little doubt they were written down; but here, again, I have failed of success in my inquiries.

This is a poor showing of native literature for all the tribes in the vast area of the United States. But, except some orations and poems, hereafter to be mentioned, it is almost all that I can name. Passing southward the harvest becomes richer. When Bishop Landa, in Yucatan, and Bishop Zumarraga, in Mexico, made bonfires, in the public squares of Mani and Tlaltilulco, of the priceless literary treasures of the Mayas and Aztecs, their maps, their parchment rolls, their calendars on wood, their painted paper books, their inscribed histories, it is recorded that the natives bewailed bitterly this obliteration of their sciences and their archives.[21] Some of them set to work to recover the memories thus doomed to oblivion, and to write them out, as best they could.

Most fertile of these were those who wrote in the Nahuatl tongue, otherwise known as the Aztec or Mexican, this being most widely spoken in Mexico, and the first cultivated by the missionaries. Many of these memoirs were short descriptions of towns or tribes, with their traditional histories. Others narrated the customs and mythologies of the race before the arrival of the whites. None were printed, and little or no care was taken to collect or preserve the manuscripts, so that probably most of them were destroyed. At length, in 1736-45, an enthusiastic Italian archaeologist, the Chevalier Lorenzo Boturini Benaduci, devoted nearly ten years to collecting everything of the kind which would throw light on ancient Mexican history. He was quite successful, and his library, had it been preserved intact, would have been to-day an invaluable source of information. But the jealous Spanish government threw Boturini into prison; his library was scattered and partly lost, and he died of chagrin and disappointment. Yet to him we probably owe the preservation of the writings of Ixtlilxochitl, Tezozomoc, and others who wrote in Spanish, and whose volumes have since seen the light in the collections of Bustamente, Lord Kingsborough, Ternaux-Compans, and elsewhere.

The Nahuatl MSS. have remained unedited. Few took an interest in their contents, fewer still in the language. The science of linguistics is very modern, and that even so perfect an idiom as the Nahuatl could command the attention of scholars for its own sake, had not dawned on the minds of patrons of learning.

Boturini catalogues some forty or fifty more or less fragmentary anonymous MSS. in Nahuatl, which he had gathered together.[22] I shall recall only those whose authors he names. Some three or four historical works were written in Nahuatl by Don Domingo de San Anton Munon Chimalpain, whom I have already mentioned as an author in Spanish also. Of his Nahuatl works his *Cronica Mexicana*, which traces the history of his nation from 1068 to 1597, would be the most worthy an editor's labors. It is now in the possession of M. Aubin.

The *Cronica de la muy noble y leal Ciudad de Tlaxcallan*, by Don Juan Ventura Zapata y Mendoza, cacique of Quiahuiztlan, extends from the earliest times to the year 1689. A copy of it, I have some reason to think, is in Mexico. Boturini possessed the original, and it should, by all means, be sought out and printed.

The ancient history of the same city was also treated of by one of the earliest native writers, and his work, in Nahuatl, alleged to have been translated by the interpreter Francisco de Loaysa, was obtained from the latter by Boturini.

An account of Tezcuco and its rulers, after the Conquest until 1564, was the work of a native, Juan de San Antonio; while Don Gabriel de Ayala, a native noble of that city, composed a history of the Tezcucan and Mexican events, extending from 1243 to 1562.[23]

Of the anonymous MSS. in Boturini's list, I shall mention only one, as it alone, of all his Nahuatl records, has succeeded in reaching publication. He called it a *History of the Kingdoms of Culhuacan and Mexico*. A copy of it passed to Mexico, where it was translated by the Licentiate Faustino Chimalpopocatl Galicia, but in a very imperfect and incorrect manner. The Abbe Brasseur de Bourbourg copied the original and the translation, and bestowed on the document both a new name, *Codex Chimalpopoca*, and a whimsical geological signification. In 1879, the Museo Nacional of Mexico began in their *Anales* the publication of the original text, this time under still another title, the *Anales de Cuauhtitlan*, with two translations, that of Galicia, and a new one by Profs. G. Mendoza and Felipe Sanchez Solis. Up to the present time, 1883, the work is not completed; but its signal importance to ancient history and mythology is amply indicated by the part in type.

Doubtless there were many MSS. which Boturini did not find, and there are, probably, to this day, going to dust in private and public libraries in Spain, valuable documents in the Nahuatl tongue.[24] For a long time it was supposed that the Nahuatl original of Father Bernardino de Sahagun's *History of New Spain* was lost; but at the meeting of the *Congres des Americanistes*, in Madrid, in 1881, a part of it, at least, was exhibited. This work almost belongs to aboriginal literature, for a considerable portion of it, notably the third, sixth and twelfth books, treating, respectively, of the origin of the gods, the Aztec oratory, and their ancient history, are mainly native narratives and speeches, taken down, word for word, in the original tongue. Spanish scholars could not render a greater service to American ethnology and linguistics than in the publication of this valuable monument.

There is, also, or, at any rate, there was, in the Royal Library at Madrid, a Mexican hieroglyphic work, "all painted," with a translation apparently into the Nahuatl tongue.[25] I would inquire of the learned linguists of Spain whether that document cannot be unearthed. And further, I would ask whether all trace has been lost of the writings of Don Gabriel Castaneda, Chief of Colomocho, who wrote, in Nahuatl, an account of the conquest of the Chichimecs by the Viceroy Antonio de Mendoza, in 1541. That Manuscript was last heard of in the library of the Convent of San Ildefonso, in Mexico.[26] Perhaps it would tell us who the Chichimecs were, about which there is disagreement enough among ethnologists.

Of the strictly hieroglyphic records I shall not take account. Their interpretation is yet uncertain, and, as linguistic monuments, they have, at present, no standing.

Equal, or superior, in culture, to the Aztecs were the Maya tribes. Their chief seat was in Yucatan, but they extended thence southwardly to the shores of the Pacific, and westward along the Gulf coast to the River Panuco. The language numbered about sixteen dialects, none very remote from the parent stem, which linguists identify as the Maya proper of the Yucatecan peninsula. While there are a number of verbal similarities between Maya and Nahuatl, the radicals of the two idioms and their grammatical structure are widely asunder. The Nahuatl is an excessively pliable, polysyllabic and highly synthetic tongue; the Maya is rigid, its words short, of one or two syllables generally, and is scarcely more synthetic than French. This contrast is carried out in the style of their writers. Those in Nahuatl were lovers of amplification, of flowing periods, of Ciceronian fullness; the Mayas cultivated sententious brevity, they are elliptical, often to obscurity, and may be compared rather to Tacitus, in his *Annals*, than to Cicero.

All the Maya tribes had strong literary tastes, but with characteristic tenacity they clung entirely to their native tongues; and I know not a single instance where one has left compositions in Spanish. Their language is easy to learn; to a stranger to both, Maya comes easier than Spanish, as intelligent writers in Yucatan have testified; and this aided its survival. Their passion for learning to read and write was strong, and had it been fed, instead of rigidly suppressed, there is little doubt but that they would have become a highly enlightened nation. The wretched system which smothered free thought in Spain killed it in Yucatan.[27]

The principal literary monument in the pure Maya is the collection known as "The Books of Chilan Balam." I have described this collection at length in previous publications, and shall content myself with a brief reference to it.[28] The title "Chilan Balam" means, in this connection, "the interpreting priest;" that is, the sacred official who, in the ancient religion, revealed the will of the gods. There are at least sixteen collections under this name in Maya, copies, probably, in part, of each other. Their contents may be classified under four headings:—

1. Chronology, calendars, and history, before and after the Conquest.

2. Prophecies and astrology.

3. Medical recipes and directions.

4. Christian narratives.

Of these, the last two are modern. The Christian portions are lives of saints, and prayers. The medical directions are often found separate, under the title "The Book of the Jew." Its language is modern and corrupt— *mestizado*, as the Spaniards express it.

The "Prophecies" are alleged to have been delivered one or several generations before the Conquest. Their style is extremely obscure, and many of the forms are archaic. If not genuine originals, they are unquestionably very early and faithful imitations of the oracular deliveries of the ancient Maya priests.

The historical portions include rude annals since the Conquest, and a series of Chronicles, extending back to about the third century of the Christian era. There are five versions of these, all of which I have published, with translations and copious notes, as the first volume of my "Library of Aboriginal American Literature."

Another class of Maya historical documents embraces the surveys and land titles, many of which date from the sixteenth century. I have in my possession a copy of one as far back as 1542, unquestionably the oldest monument of the Maya language extant. Sometimes these titles were accompanied by a family history. Such is "The Chronicle of Chac Xulub Chen," written by the Chief Nakuk Pech, in 1562, which I have published. It gives, in a confused style, a history of the Conquest, and throws light on the methods by which the Spaniards succeeded in overcoming the various native tribes.[29]

We owe the preservation of most of the Maya MSS. to the enlightened labors of Don Juan Pio Perez, a distinguished Yucatecan scholar, and the compiler of the best printed dictionary of the Maya tongue.[30] The most complete collection now in existence is that of the Canon Crescencio Carrillo y Ancona, a learned archaeologist, and author of an excellent history of Maya literature.[31]

After the Maya, the most important of these associated dialects was the Cakchiquel. It was, and still is, spoken in Guatemala; and the Kiche (Quiche), also current there, is so nearly allied to it that they may be treated as one idiom. The Cakchiquel possesses an extensive Christian literature, as it was cultivated assiduously by the early missionaries. Indeed, there was, for many years, a chair in the University of Guatemala created for teaching it, and it is often referred to as the *lengua metropolitana*, Guatemala having been the see of an archbishop. There are in existence extensive lexicons of Cakchiquel, and in it, besides various collections of sermons, was written the once celebrated work of Father Domingo de Vico, the *Theologia Indorum*, probably the most complete theological treatise ever produced in a native American tongue.[32]

The most notable aboriginal production in Cakchiquel is one frequently referred to by the Abbe Brasseur de Bourbourg as the *Memorial de Tecpan Atitlan*, The Records from Tecpan Atitlan.[33] It is an historical account of his family and tribe, written in the sixteenth century by a member of the junior branch of the ruling house of the Cakchiquels. His name was Don Francisco Ernantez Arana Xahila, and a passage of the MS. informs us that he was writing in 1581. After his death the work was continued by Don Francisco Tiaz Gebuta Queh. The style is familiar and often vivid, and the work is addressed to his children. It begins with the earliest myths and traditions of the tribe, and follows their fortunes to the lifetime of the writer. In respect both to mythology, history and language, it is one of the most noteworthy monuments of American antiquity. A loose paraphrase of it was made by Brasseur de Bourbourg, based upon which, a Spanish rendering was published by the "Sociedad Economica de Guatemala," under the auspices of Senor Gavarrete. Neither the original nor any correct translation has been printed.

A copy of this MS. is in my collection, and both the original and a second copy are in Europe; but there were a number of similar historical accounts, committed to writing by this people and their immediate neighbors, of which we know little but the titles and a few extracts. Thus, the historian of Guatemala, Don Domingo Juarros, quotes from the MSS. of Don Francisco Gomez, *Ahzib Kiche*, or Chief Scribe of the Kiches, of Don Francisco Garcia Calel Tzumpan, of Don Juan Macario, nephew, and Don Juan Torres, son, of the Chief Chignavincelut, and "the histories written by the Quiches, Cakchiquels, Pipils, Pocomans, and others, who learned to write their tongues from their Spanish teachers." These MSS. gave the genealogies of their families and the migrations of their ancestors "from the time when the Toltecs, from whom they trace descent, first entered the territory of Mexico, and found it inhabited by the Chichimecs."[34]

One of the motives prompting to the composition of these works was to vindicate the claims of families to the sovereignty, or to the possession of land. They were, in fact, a sort of briefs of titles to real estate. One such is preserved, in the original, in the Brasseur collection, and is catalogued as "The Royal Title of Don Francisco Izquin, the last Ahpop Galel, or King, of Nehaib, granted by the lords who invested him with his royal dignity, and confirmed by the last King of Quiche, with other sovereigns, November 22, 1558."[35] A Spanish translation of the title of a female branch of this same family was printed at Guatemala in 1876, but the original text has never been put to press, although it is said to be still preserved in one of the ancient families of the Province of Totonicapam.[36]

Another Kiche work, which has excited a lively but not very intelligent interest among European scholars, is the *Popol Vuh*, National Book, a compendious account of their mythology and traditional history. A Spanish translation of it by Father Francisco Ximenez was edited in Vienna, in 1857, by Dr. Carl Scherzer.[37] The Abbe Brasseur followed, in 1861, by a publication of the original text, and a new translation into French.[38] This text fills 173 octavo pages, so that it will be seen that it offers an ample specimen of the tongue.

Neither of these translations is satisfactory. Ximenez wrote with all the narrow prejudices of a Spanish monk, while Brasseur was a Euhemerist of the most advanced type, and saw in every myth the statement of a historical fact. There is need of a re-translation of the whole, with critical linguistic notes attached. A few years ago, I submitted the names and epithets of the divinities mentioned in the Popol Vuh to a careful analysis, and I think the results obtained show clearly how erroneous were the conceptions formed regarding them by both the translators of the document.[39] I shall not here go into the question of its age or authorship, about which diverse opinions have obtained; but I will predict that the more sedulously it is studied, the more certainly it will be shown to be a composition inspired by ideas and narratives familiar to the native mind long before the advent of Christianity.

I have been told that there are other versions of the *Popol Vuh* still preserved among the Kiches, and it were ardently to be desired that they were sought out, as there are many reasons to believe that the copy we have is incomplete, or, at any rate, omits some prominent features of their mythology.

One branch of the Maya race, the Tzendals, inhabited a portion of the province of Chiapas. One of their hero-gods bore the name of *Votan*, a word from a Maya root, signifying the breast or heart, but from its faint resemblance to "Odin," and its still fainter similarity to "Buddha," their myth about him has given rise to many whimsical speculations. This myth was written down in the native tongue by a Christianized native, in the seventeenth century. The MS. came into the possession of Nunez de la Vega, Bishop of Chiapas, who quotes from it in his *Constituciones Diocesanas*, printed in Rome, in 1702. The indefatigable Boturini tells us that he tried in vain to find it, about 1740, and supposed it was lost.[40] But a copy of it was seen and described by Dr. Paul Felix Cabrera, in 1790.[41] Possibly it is still in existence, and there are few fragments of American literature which would better merit a diligent search. As to the meaning of the Votan myth, I have ventured an explanation of it in another work.[42]

In South America, the only native historical writers who employed their own tongue appear to have been of the Peruvian Qquichua stock. None of their productions have been published, but one or more are in existence and accessible. Prominent among them and deserving of early editing by competent hands, is an anonymous treatise, partly translated by Dr. Francisco de Avila, in 1608, on the "Errors, False Gods, Superstitions and Diabolical Rites" of the natives of the provinces of Huarochiri, Mama and Chaclla. The original text is in Madrid, and Avila's translation, as far as it goes, has been rendered into English by Mr. Clements R. Markham, and published in one of the Hackluyt Society's volumes.[43]

A member of the Inca family, already referred to, Don Luis Inca, is reported to have written a series of historical notes, *Advertencias*, "with his own hand and in his own tongue;" but what became of his manuscript is not known.[44]

There is another class of historical documents, which profess to be the production of native hands, and which are moderately numerous. These are the official letters and petitions drawn up by the chiefs in their own tongues, and forwarded to the Spanish authorities. Of these, two interesting specimens, one in the "Abolachi" tongue (a dialect of Muskokee), and the other in Timucuana, were published in fac-simile by the late Mr. Buckingham Smith, but in a very limited number of copies (only fifty in all). Others in

Nahuatl and Maya, also in fac-simile, appear in that magnificent volume, the *Cartas de Indias*, issued by the Spanish Government in 1880. Doubtless more examples could be found in the public Archives in Spain, and they should all be collected into one volume. They were probably prompted by the Spanish local authorities; but it is likely that they show the true structure of the language, and, of course, they have a positive historical value.

It is related in the Proceedings of the Municipal Council of Guatemala that, in 1692, the Captain Antonio de Fuentes y Guzman laid before the Council seven petitions, written in the native language, on the bark of trees.[45] Whatever of interest they contained was, no doubt, extracted by that laborious but imaginative writer, and included in his *History*, which has never been published, though several manuscript copies of it are in existence.

It will be seen that some of the so-called historical literature I have mentioned rests uncertain on the border line between fact and fancy. These old stories may be vague memories of past deeds, set in a frame of mythical details; or they may be ancient myths, solar or meteorological, which came to receive credence as actual occurrences. The task remains for special students of such matters to sift and analyze them, and settle this debateable point.

There is another class of narrations, about which there can be no doubt as to their purely imaginative origin. These are the animal myths, the fairy stories, the fireside tales of giants and magicians, with which the hours of leisure are whiled away. Several collections of these have been made, the words and phrases taken down precisely as the native story-teller delivered them, and thus they come strictly within the lines of aboriginal literature. They are the spontaneous outgrowth of the native mind, and are faithful examples of native speech.

Over a hundred such tales have been collected by Dr. Couto de Magalhaes, as narrated by the Tupis of Brazil, and many of them have been published with all desirable fidelity, and with a philosophical introduction and notes, in a volume issued by the Brazilian government, under his editorial care.[46]

A similar collection of Tupi stories was made by the late Prof. Charles F. Hartt, whose early death was a loss to more than one branch of science. It was his intention to edit them with the necessary notes and vocabularies; but, so far as I know, the only specimens which appeared in print were those he laid before the American Philological Association, in 1872.[47] The inquiries I have instituted about his MSS. have not been successful.

Numerous texts of this description have been obtained from the Klamath Indians by Mr. A.S. Gatschet, and from the Omaha by the Rev. J. Owen Dorsey, both of which collections are in process of publication by the Bureau of Ethnology at Washington. Scattered specimens of stories of this kind have also been obtained by a number of travelers, and they are always a welcome aid to the study both of the psychology and language of a tribe.

Section 4.
Didactic Literature

The more civilized American tribes had made considerable advances in some of the natural sciences, and in none more than in practical astronomy. By close observation of the heavenly bodies they had elaborated a complicated and remarkably exact system of chronology. They had determined the length of the year with greater accuracy than the white invaders; and the different cycles by which they computed time allowed them to assign dates to occurrences many hundreds of years anterior.

Although there are local differences, the calendars in use in Central and Southern Mexico and in Central America were evidently derived from one and the same original. A great deal has been written upon them, but for all that many questions about them remain unanswered. We do not know the Maya method of intercalation; we do not understand the uses of the shorter Mexican year, of 260 days; we are at a loss to explain the purpose of doubling the length of certain months, as prevailed among the Cakchiquels; we are in the dark about the significance of the names of many days and months; we cannot see why the nations chose to begin the count of the year at different seasons; and there are ever so many more knotty problems about this remarkable system and its variations.

What we imperatively need is a supply of authentic aboriginal calendars, accurately reproduced, for purposes of comparison. Boturini collected a number of these, which he describes, and long before his day some specimens had been published by Valades and Gemelli Carreri.[48] They were, in ancient times, usually depicted by circular drawings, called by the Spaniards, Wheels (*ruedas*). After the Conquest they were written out, more in the form of our almanacs. One such, in the Maya tongue, with a translation, was contributed to Mr. Stephens' *Travels in Yucatan*, by the eminent Maya scholar, Don Juan Pio Perez.[49] Several others were in his collection, and are accessible. Dr. Berendt succeeded in securing *fac similes* of Kiche and Cakchiquel calendars, written out in the seventeenth century, and these are now in my possession. I fear we have no perfect examples of the Zapotec calendar, nor of that of the Tarascos of Michoacan, although an anonymous author, most of whose MS. has been preserved, reduced the latter to writing, and it may some day turn up.[50] The Aztec calendars collected by Boturini would, were they published, give us sufficient material, probably, to understand clearly the methods of that tribe.

One momentous purpose which the calendar served was for supplying omens and predictions; another was for the appointment of fasts and festivals, for the religious ritual. The calendar arranged for these objects was called, in the Nahuatl, *tonalamatl*, "the book of days," and in Maya *tzolante*, "that by which events are arranged." So intimately were all the acts of individual and national life bound up with these superstitions, that an understanding of them is indispensable to a successful study of the psychology and history of the race.

After the Conquest some of the notions about judicial astrology, then prevalent in Europe, crept into the native understanding, and notably, in the *Books of Chilan Balam* we find forecastes of lucky and unlucky days, and discussions of planetary influence, evidently borrowed from the Spanish almanacs of the seventeenth century.

Most of the Aborigines of the Continent possessed a keen sense of locality, and often a certain rude skill in cartography. The relative position of spots and proportionate distances were approximately represented by rough drawings. They knew the boundaries of their lands, the courses of streams, the trend of shores, and could display them intelligently. These maps, as they are called, present a very different appearance from ours. Those of the Aztecs are rather pictured diagrams, something like those we find in fifteenth century books of travel. A fair specimen, though of date later than the Conquest, was published not long since, in Madrid.[51]

The Maya maps are even more conventional. A central point is taken, usually a town, around which is drawn either a circle or a square, on the four sides of which are placed the figures of the four cardinal points, and within the figures are the various symbols which denote the villages, wells, ponds, and other objects which are to be designated. Specimens of some of these, all after the Conquest, however, have been published by Mr. Stephens and Canon Carrillo,[52] and others are found in the various *Books of Chilan Balam*.

Very few strictly scholastic works seem to have been produced by the natives. Nearly all those which I have seen for use in the Mission schools appear to be the productions of the white instructors, generally, of course, aided by some intelligent native. I have in my possession an *Ortografia en Lengua Kekchi*, picked up by Dr. Berendt in Vera Paz, which was the work of Domingo Coy, an Indian of Coban (MS. pp. 32). But on examination it proves to be merely an adaptation of a *Manual de Ortografia Castellana*, in use in the schools, and not an original effort. For all that, it is not without linguistic value. In Mexico a useful little book of instruction in Nahuatl has been prepared by the licentiate Faustino Chimalpopoca Galicia, a scholar of indigenous extraction.[53] An older work, of a similar character, by Don Antonio Tobar, a descendant of the Montezumas, is mentioned by bibliographers, but never was printed, and has probably perished.[54]

It has always been part of the policy of both Catholic and Protestant missions to permit the natives to enter the career of the church; in the territories of both confessions instances are moderately numerous of priests and preachers of half or full Indian blood. Most of these educated men, however, rather shunned the cultivation of their maternal tongues, and preferred, when they wrote at all, to choose that of their white brethren, the Spanish, Portuguese or English. The extensive theological literature which we possess, printed or in manuscript, in American tongues, and in many it is quite ample, is scarcely ever the result of the efforts of the Christian teachers of indigenous affiliations.

A notable exception was the licentiate Bartolome de Alva, a native Mexican, descended from the Tezcucan kings, who composed, in Nahuatl and Spanish, a *Confessionario*, which was printed at Mexico in 1634. It contains some interesting references to the mythology and superstitions of the natives.[55]

The Indian Elias Boudinot and other Cherokees have printed many essays and tracts in that tongue, but whether original or merely translated I do not know. The sermons of the native Protestant missionaries to their fellows were probably extempore addresses. At any rate, I have not seen any in manuscript or print. A volume of the kind exists, however, in manuscript, in the Library of the *Instituto Historico* of Rio Janeiro, which it would be very desirable to have printed. It is the *Sermones e Exemplos em lengua Guarani*, by Nicolas Japuguay, cura of the Parish of San Francisco in 1727.[56] But when it is edited, let us hope that it will be a more favorable example of critical care than the *Crestomathia da Lingua Brasilica*, edited by Dr. Ernesto Ferreira Franca (Leipzig, 1859), which, according to Professor Hartt, is "badly arranged, carelessly edited, and disfigured by innumerable typographical errors."[57]

A curious variety of religious literature is what are called the Passions, *Las Pasiones*, which are found among the natives of the Isthmus of Tehuantepec. These prose chants took their rise at an early period among the sodalities (*cofradias*), organized under the name of some particular saint. Each of these societies possessed a volume, called its Regulations (*Ordenanzas*), containing, among other matters, a series of invocations, founded on the history of the Passion of Christ. During Holy Week, certain members of the fraternity, called *fiscales*, gather in the church, around one of their number, who reads a sentence in a loud voice. The fiscales repeat it in a chanting tone, with a uniform and monotonous cadence. It is probable that these chants are the compositions of the Indians themselves. Dr. Berendt obtained several copies of these, some in the Chapaneca of Chiapas, and others in the Zoque of the Isthmus, which are now in my hands.

Section 5.
Oratorical Literature

The love of the American Indian for oratorical display has been commented on by almost all writers who have studied his disposition. Specimens of native eloquence have been introduced into school books, and declaimed by many an aspiring young Cicero. Most of them are, doubtless, as fictitious as Logan's celebrated speech, which was exalted by the great Jefferson almost to a level with the outbursts of Demosthenes, to be reduced again to very small proportions by the criticisms of Brantz Mayer.[58]

In fact, in spite of all that has been said about the native oratory, we are in a very inadequate position to judge of it correctly, and this because we have no accurate reports in the original tongues of their speeches. Translations, more or less loose, more or less imaginary, we have in abundance; but, for critical purposes, they are simply worthless.

Yet that even the ruder tribes in both the northern and southern continents, attached great weight to the cultivation of oratory, is amply evident. James Adair, who is competent authority, tells us that the southern Indians studied public speaking assiduously, and that their speeches "abound with bolder tropes and figures than illiterate interpreters can well comprehend or explain."[59] Mr. Howse writes that, among the Crees, those who possess oratorical talent are in demand by the Chiefs, who employ them to deliver the official harangues.[60] Among the Aztecs, the very word for chief, *tlatoani*, literally means "orator" (from the verb *tlatoa*, to harangue). In the far south, among the Araucanians of Chili, and their relatives the migratory hordes of the Pampas, no gift is in higher estimation than that of an easy and perspicuous delivery. This alone enables the humblest to rise to the position of chieftain.[61] So it was over the whole continent.

In most of their languages, the oratorical was markedly different from the familiar or colloquial style. The former was given to antithesis, repetition, elaborate figures, unusual metaphors, and more sonorous and lengthened expressions. The Rev. Mr. Byington gives a number of the oratorical affectations in the Choctaw, as *akakano* for *ak*, *okakocha* for *ok*, etc. [62]

Some genuine specimens of the oratory of the northern tribes are preserved by Mr. Hale, in the Iroquois *Book of Rites*, to which I have referred on a previous page. The speeches it contains were learned by heart, and transmitted from generation to generation, long before they were committed to writing, and long after some of the words and expressions they contain had become lost to the colloquial language of the tribe.

The ancient Mexicans were much given to this sort of formal speech-making. They had a large number of cut-and-dried orations, which professional rhetoricians delivered on all important occasions in life. The new-born child was harangued at, in good set terms, when it was but a few days old. Betrothals, marriages, festivals, the commencement of puberty and of pregnancy, etc., were all celebrated by the delivery of discourses. Fathers taught their children, teachers their pupils, monarchs their vassals, war chiefs their soldiers, by such declamations. The general name for these speeches was *huehuetlatolli*, ancient orations.[63]

Many have been preserved, and a tolerably complete collection could be made in the original tongue. To effect this, we should have to have recourse to the original Nahuatl MS. of Sahagun's history, which, I have already said, exists in Madrid; next, to the extremely rare work of the eminent Nahuatl scholar, Father Juan Baptista, *Platicas Morales*, in which, according to Vetancurt, he gives, in the original, the ancient addresses of fathers to their children, and of rulers to their subjects;[64] and lastly, to the recently published, though very early written, *Mexican Grammar*, of the Franciscan Andre de Olmos, which contains a number of these discourses, carefully edited and translated by the accomplished scholar, M. Remi Simeon.[65]

The numerous prayers to the heathen gods, preserved by Sahagun, are, doubtless, faithfully recorded, and are accurate examples of the elevated literary style of the ancient Aztecs. They should, by all means, be printed, so that they could be accessible to those who would acquaint themselves with the genius of the language and the psychology of the people.

In the Qquichua of Peru, a few similar prayers to Viracocha have been saved from oblivion, in the pages of Cristobal de Molina. One or more copies of his *Relacion* are in the United States, but it has only appeared in print through a translation by Mr. Markham, in the Hackluyt Society's publications.[66] Some modern prayers of the Mayas are to be found in the collection of Brasseur,[67] and, doubtless, several of the so-called ancient "prophecies," preserved in the *Books of Chilan Balam*, are, in fact, specimens of the impassioned and mystic rhapsodies with which the priests of their heathendom entertained their hearers, as Cortes and his followers heard, one day, on the island of Cozumel.[68]

Section 6.
Poetical Literature

Man, remarks Wilhelm von Humboldt, belongs to the singing species of animals. True it is, that wherever found, he has some notion of music, cultivates the accord of sounds by some sort of instrument, and gives expression to his most acute emotions in modulations of vocal tone.

The earliest and simplest poetry is nothing more than such modulated sounds; it is not in definite words, and hence, is not capable of translation; it is but the expression of feeling through the voice, as is the wail of the infant, the rippling laughter of youth, the crooning of senility, the groans of pain or sorrow.

Perhaps this first is also the highest expression of the aesthetic sense. The most admired cantatrices of to-day drown the words in a wealth of vocalization, and the meaning is lost, even were the language one known to their hearers, which it usually is not. I have heard a living poet, himself of no mean eminence, maintain that the harmony of versification is a far higher test of true poetic power than the ideas conveyed.

These principles must be borne in mind when we apply the canons of criticism to the poetry of the ruder races. It is not composed to be read, or even recited, but to be sung; its aim is, not to awaken thought or convey information, but solely to excite emotion. It can have a meaning only when heard, and only in the surroundings which gave it birth.

Hence it is, that the notices of the poetry of American nations are so scant and unsatisfactory. While all travelers agree that the tribes have songs and chants, war songs, peace songs, love songs, and others, few satisfactory specimens have been recorded. Those who have examined the subject most accurately have found that many so-called songs are mere repetitions of a few words, or even of simple interjections, over and over again, with an endless iteration, in a chanting voice. The Dakota songs which have been preserved by Riggs, the Chippeway songs obtained from the interpreter Tanner, and the numerous specimens of native Californian chants recorded by Powers, as well as many others of this class which might be mentioned, are mainly of this character.

Consequently, they show very poorly in a translation, and are apt to convey an unjustly depreciatory notion of the nations which produce them. To estimate them aright, the meter and the music must be taken into consideration, and also their suitability to the minds to which they were addressed.[69]

But the anthology of America is not limited to specimens of this kind. In the Iroquois *Book of Rites* there are funeral dirges of considerable length, expressive and touching in meaning; and in the Algonkin a few have been preserved in the original, which are authentic and pleasing. Here, for instance, is a nearly literal version of a Chippeway love song:—

> "I will walk into somebody's dwelling,
> Into somebody's dwelling will I walk.
>
> To thy dwelling, my dearly beloved,
> Some night will I walk, will I walk.
>
> Some night in the winter, my beloved,
> To thy dwelling will I walk, will I walk.
>
> This very night, my beloved,
> To thy dwelling will I walk, will I walk."[70]

Much more striking, and to me strangely so, are the songs of the Taensa, a small tribe who dwelt on the banks of the lower Mississippi. They are now extinct, but a very curious account of their language, by a Spanish missionary, has been preserved and recently published. The early travelers speak of them as an unusually cultivated people, but one cannot but be surprised to find them capable of composing an epithalamium like the following:—

"Tikaens, thou buildest a house, thou bringest thy wife to live in it.

"Thou art married, Tikaens, thou art married.

"Thou wilt become famous; thy children will name thee among the elders. Think of Tikaens as an old man!

"By what name is thy bride known? Is she beautiful? Are her eyes soft as the light of the moon? Is she a strong woman? Didst thou understand her signs during the dance?

"I know not whether thou lovest her, Tikaens.

"What said the old man, her father, when thou askedst for his pretty daughter?

"What betrothal presents didst thou give?

"Rejoice, Tikaens! be glad, be happy!

"Build thyself a happy home.

"This is the song of its building!"

Some of the songs of war and death are quite Ossianic in style, and yet they appear to be accurate translations.[71]

The comparatively elevated style of such poems need not cast doubt upon them. The first European who wrote about the songs of the natives of America, who was none other than the witty and learned Montaigne, paid a high tribute to their true poetic spirit. Montaigne knew a man who had lived among the Tupis of Brazil for ten or twelve years, and had learned their language and customs. He remembered several of their songs of war and love, and translated them to gratify the insatiable thirst for knowledge of the famous essayist. The refrain of one of them, supposed to be addressed to one of those beautiful serpents of the tropical forests, ran thus:—

"O serpent, stay! stay, O serpent! that thy painted skin may serve my sister as a pattern for the design and form of a rich cord, which I may give to my love; for this favor, may thy beauty and grace be esteemed beyond those of all other serpents."

"I have had enough to do with poetry," comments Montaigne on this couplet, "to say about this that not only is there nothing barbarous in this fancy, but that it is altogether worthy of Anacreon." Such is his enthusiasm, indeed, that he finds in this simple and faithful expression of sentiment the highest form of poesy; "the true, the supreme, the divine; that which is above rules and beyond reasoning."[72]

Scarcely can we call these words extravagant, when, in our own century, another Frenchman, eminent as a scientific observer, and speaking from the results of personal study on the spot, has said of the songs of a tribe of this same Tupi stock, the Guarayos, that they cannot be surpassed for grace of language and delicacy of expression.[73]

Many interesting Klamath, Omaha and Zuni verses have been collected by the efforts of Gatschet, Dorsey, Cushing and other zealous laborers connected with the Bureau of Ethnology at Washington, and these will shortly be accessible to all through the accurate publications of the government press.

The melodious Nahuatl tongue lent itself readily to poetic composition, and was cultivated enthusiastically in this direction long before the Conquest. Apparently the poetic dialect never freed itself from the use of unmeaning particles thrown in to complete the meter; as, indeed, may also be said of the English popular song dialect, which retains to this day very many such.[74]

With this exception the Tezcucan poets, for it was in that province that the muses were most assiduously worshiped, made use of a pure, brilliant, figurative style, and had developed a large variety of metrical forms.

One of the most famous disciples of the lyre was Nezahualcoyotl, himself sovereign of Tezcuco about the year 1460. He left seventy odes on philosophical and religious subjects, which were borne in memory and repeated after the Conquest. Translations of a few of them have come down to us, but my inquiries as to the whereabouts of the originals, if, indeed, they exist, have been fruitless.[75] The Jesuit, Horatio Carochi, published some ancient verses in his grammar of the Nahuatl (Mexico, 1645). Several which appear in later works do not seem to merit the credit of antiquity. They are more like those which Sahagun wrote and published, in Nahuatl, at a very early period,[76] Christian songs, intended to take the place of the ditties of love and chants of war, which the natives had such a passion for singing.

Under the title *Cantares de los Mexicanos*, there was long preserved in the library of the University of Mexico a manuscript of the sixteenth or seventeenth century, with a large number of supposed ancient Aztec songs; but what has become of it now, nobody knows.[77] Thus it is that these precious monuments of antiquity are allowed to lie uncared for, through generations, until, at length, they fall a prey to ignorance or theft.

A few other fragments of Nahuatl poetry, all probably modern, but some of them the versification of native bards, might be named; but the whole of it, as now existing, could give us but a faint idea of the perfection to which the art appears to have attained in the palmy days of the great Tezcucan poet-prince.

In the literature of the Maya group of dialects, there have been preserved various sacred chants, some in the *Books of Chilan Balam*, others in the Kiche *Popol Vuh*. What are known as the "Maya Prophecies" are, as I have said, evidently the originals, or echoes of the mystic songs of the priests of Kukulkan and Itzamna, deities of the Maya pantheon, who were supposed to inspire their devotees with the power of foretelling the future.

The modern Maya lends itself very readily both to rhyme and rhythm, and I have in my possession some quite neat specimens of versification in it, from the pen of the Yucatecan historian, Apolinar Garcia y Garcia.

When we reach Peru we find a race not less poetical in temperament than the cultured Mexicans. Nothing but their ignorance of an alphabet, and the indifference or fanatical hatred of the early explorers for the productions of the native intellect, prevented the perpetuation of a Qquichua literature, both extensive and noble. As it is, we may expect many valuable examples of it when the learned Peruvian scholar, Senor Gavino Pacheco Zegarra, shall publish his long promised *Tresor de la Langue des Incas*. Among them he has announced the first appearance of a number of *Yaravis*, or elegiac chants, composed by the Indians themselves, and sung in memory of their departed friends.

We know, from the testimony of Garcillaso de la Vega, that the Inca bards formed a separate and highly respected class, and that in their hands the supple Qquichua tongue had been brought under well recognized rules of prosody. He mentions the different classes and subjects of their poems, compares them to similar compositions in Spanish, and even gives specimens of two short ones, of undoubted antiquity, and adds that, when a boy, he knew many others. "What would not one now give," exclaims Mr. Markham, "for those precious relics of Inca civilization, which the half-caste lad allowed to slip from his memory."[78] All that Mr. Markham could collect, in his extensive journeys in Peru, were not above twenty songs of ancient date, and I regret to say that these have not yet been published.

Of those charming Tupi songs, to which I have already referred, I fear that we have but very few preserved in the original tongue. Not that there is any lack of poems in the *lingoa geral*, or "common language" of Brazil, as the ordinary and corrupt Tupi there spoken is called. It is a melodious idiom, lending itself easily to rhyme and rhythm, and several Brazilian writers of European blood have gained reputation by their compositions in it. But of genuine aboriginal productions, there are not many.

The entertaining old voyager, Jean de Lery, who visited Brazil with Villegagnon in 1557, has recorded a few simple airs, which appear to be merely choruses or refrains of songs, the delivery of which was, however, so effective, that to hear them carried him out of himself; and ever, when his memory recalled them, his heart beat, and it seemed that he heard the wild cadence once again resounding in his ears through the tropical forests.[79]

Some strange old poetic invocations in archaic Tupi addressed to the moon and to the god of love, Ruda, who dwells in the clouds, have been collected and printed by Dr. Couto de Magalhaes, a writer whose studies on Tupi poetry, its character and development, merit high praise.[80] Both the songs and music of the modern natives of that country attracted the attention of the learned Von Martius, and in his volumes of *Travels in Brazil* an appendix is devoted to their discussion.[81] Many excellent hints for preparing a Tupi anthology are also contained in an erudite note of Ferdinand Denis to his description of the visit of fifty native Tupis to France, in 1550.[82]

Section 7.
Dramatic Literature

The development of the dramatic art can be clearly traced in the American nations. When the Spaniards first explored the West Indian Islands they found the inhabitants much given to festivals which combined dancing with chanting, and the introduction of figures with peculiar costumes. The native name of these representations was adopted by the Spaniards, and applied to such performances elsewhere. The word is *areytos*, and is derived from the Arawack verb, *aririn*, to rehearse, recite.[83]

Such dramatic recitations were found among most of the tribes of North and South America, and have been frequently described by travelers. Often they were of a religious nature, having something to do with devotional exercises; but not seldom they were simply for amusement. Occasionally they were mere pantomimes, where the actors appeared in costume and masks, and went through some ludicrous scene. Thus, to quote one example out of many, Lieutenant Timberlake saw some among the Cherokees, about the middle of the last century, which he speaks of as "very diverting," where some of the actors dressed in the skins of wild animals, and the simulated contest between these pretended beasts and the men who hunted them, were the motives of the entertainment.[84]

From the solemn religious representations on the one hand and these diverting masquerades on the other, arose the two forms of tragedy and comedy, both of which were widely popular among the American aborigines.[85] The effete notion that they were either unimaginative or insusceptible to humor is, to be sure, still retained by a few writers, who are either ignorant or prejudiced; but it has been refuted so often that I need not stop to attack it. In fact, so many tribes were of a gay and frolicsome disposition, so much given to joking, to playing on words, and to noticing the humorous aspect of occurrences, that they have not unfrequently been charged by the whites best acquainted with them, the missionaries, with levity and a frivolous temperament.

Among the many losses which American ethnology has suffered, that of the text of the native dramas is one of the most regretable. Is is, however, not total. Two have been published which claim to be, and I think are, faithful renditions of the ancient texts as they were transmitted verbally, from one to another, in pre-Columbian times.

The most celebrated of these is the drama of *Ollanta*,[86] in the Qquichua language of Peru. No less than eight editions of this have been published, the last and best of which is that by the meritorious scholar, Senor Gavino Pacheco Zegarra. The internal evidence of the antiquity of this drama has been pronounced conclusive by all competent Qquichua students.[87]

The plot is varied and ingenious, and the characters agreeably contrasted. Ollanta is a warrior of low degree, who falls in love with Cusi Coyllur, daughter of the Inca, who returns his affection. The lovers have secret meetings, and Ollanta asks the sovereign to sanction their union. The proud ruler rejects the proposal with scorn, and the audacious warrior gathers his adherents and attacks the State, at first with success. But Cusi Coyllur is thrown into prison and her child, the fruit of her illicit love, is separated from her. The Inca dies, and under his successor Ollanta is defeated and brought, a prisoner, to the capital. Mindful, however, of his merits, the magnanimous victor pardons him, restores him to his honors, and returns to his arms Cusi Coyllur and her child. Minor characters are a facetious youth, who is constantly punning and joking; and the dignified figure of the High Priest of the Sun, who endeavors to dissuade the hero from his seemingly hopeless love.

The second drama to which I refer is that of *Rabinal Achi*, in the Kiche tongue of Guatemala. The text was obtained by the Abbe Brasseur de Bourbourg, and edited with a French translation. The plot is less complete than that of the *Ollanta*, and the constant repetitions, while they constitute strong evidence of its antiquity and native origin, are tedious to a European reader.[88]

Rabinal-Achi is a warrior who takes captive a distinguished foe, Canek, and brings him before the ruler of Rabinal, King Hobtoh. The fate of the prisoner is immediate death and he knows it, but his audacity and bravery do not fail him. He boasts of his warlike exploits, and taunts his captors, like an Iroquois in his death song, and his enemies listen with respect. He even threatens the king, and has to be restrained from attacking him. As his end draws near, he asks to drink from the royal cup and eat from the royal dish; it is granted. Again, he asks to be clothed in the royal robe; it is brought and put about him. Once more he makes a request, and it is to kiss the virgin mouth of the daughter of the king, and dance a measure with her, "as the last sign of his death and his end." Even this is conceded, and one might think that it was his uttermost petition. But no; he asks one year's grace, wherein to bid adieu to his native mountains. The king hears this in silence, and Canek disappears; but returning in a moment, he scornfully inquires whether they supposed he had run away. He then, in a few strong words, bids a last farewell to his bow, his shield, his war-club and battle-axe, and is slain by the warriors of the king.

The love of dramatic performances was not crushed out in the natives by the Conquest. In fact, in the Spanish countries, it was turned to account and cultivated by the missionaries as a means of instructing their converts in religion, by "miracle plays" or *autos sacramentales*, as they are called. It was even permitted to the more intelligent natives to compose the text of plays. One such, manifestly, I think, the work of a native author, in the mixed Nahuatl-Spanish dialect of Nicaragua, I have prepared for publication. The original was found by Dr. Berendt in Masaya, and his copy, without note or translation, came into my hands.

The play is a light comedy, and is called "The Ballet of the Gueegueence or the Macho-Raton." The characters are a wily old rascal, Gueegueence, and his two sons, the one a chip of the old block, the other a bitter commentator on the family failings. They are brought before the Governor for entering his province without a permit; but by bragging and promises the foxy old man succeeds both in escaping punishment and in effecting a marriage between his scapegrace son and the Governor's daughter. The interest is not in the plot, which is trivial, but in the constant play on words, and in the humor, often highly Rabelaisian, of the anything but venerable parent.

The "Zacicoxol," or Drama of Cortes and Montezuma, written in Kiche, of which I have a copy, may possibly be the work of an Indian, but is probably largely that of one of the Spanish curas, and appears to have little in it of interest.

Another and peculiar form of dramatic recitation is what are called the Loas or *Logas*, of Central America. In these, a single individual appears in some quaint costume, in a little theatre erected for the purpose, and recites a burlesque poem, acting the different portions of it to the best of his ability. At present, most of these *Logas* are of a semi-religious character. The one I have is entitled "The Loga of the Child-God," *Loga del nino Dios*, and is written in Spanish intermingled with words from the Mangue or Chorotegan language. This tongue, spoken by a few persons in Nicaragua, is closely akin to the Chapanec of Chiapas, and was a sonorous and rich idiom. Those who spoke it were much given to scenic representations, as we learn from the historian Oviedo, who lived among them for nearly a year, about 1527. None of these remain, though as late as about 1820, one of great antiquity, believed to be an original native production, continued to be acted. Its title was *La Ollita* or *El Canahuate*, the former word meaning the peculiar musical instrument of that locality, the "whistling jar." The subject was a tale of love, and one of these primitive flutes was used as an accompaniment to the songs.

Section 8.
Conclusion

Thus do I answer the questions which I proposed at the outset of my thesis. If I have failed to justify the expectations which I may have raised, at least I have thrown into strong relief the cause of my failure, to wit, the utter and incredible neglect which, up to this hour, has prevailed with regard to the preservation of what relics of native literature which we know have existed,—which do still exist.

Time and money are spent in collecting remains in wood and stone, in pottery and tissue and bone, in laboriously collating isolated words, and in measuring ancient constructions. This is well, for all these things teach us what manner of men made up the indigenous race, what were their powers, their aspirations, their mental grasp. But closer to very self, to thought and being, are the connected expressions of men in their own tongues. The monuments of a nation's literature are more correct mirrors of its mind than any merely material objects. I have at least shown that there are some such, which have been the work of native American authors. My object is to engage in their preservation and publication the interest of scholarly men, of learned societies, of enlightened governments, of liberal institutions and individuals, not only in my own country, but throughout the world. Science is cosmopolitan, and the study of man is confined by no geographical boundaries. The languages of America and the literary productions in those languages have every whit as high a claim on the attention of European scholars as have the venerable documents of Chinese lore, the mysterious cylinders of Assyria, or the painted and figured papyri of the Nilotic tombs.

* * * * *

FOOTNOTES:

[Footnote 1: What Dr. Washington Matthews says of one of the Sioux tribes is, in substance, true of all on the Continent:—

"Long winter evenings are often passed in reciting and listening to stories of various kinds. Some of these are simply the accounts given by the men, of their own deeds of valor, their hunts and journeys; some are narrations of the wonderful adventures of departed heroes; while many are fictions, full of impossible incidents, of witchcraft and magic. The latter class of stories are very numerous. Some of them have been handed down through many generations; some are of recent origin; while a few are borrowed from other tribes. Some old men acquire great reputation as story tellers, and are invited to houses, and feasted, by those who are desirous of listening to them. Good story tellers often originate tales, and do not disclaim the authorship. When people of different tribes meet they often exchange tales with one another. An old Indian will occupy several hours in telling a tale, with much elegant and minute description."—*Ethnography and Philology of the Hidatsa Indians*, pp. 62-3. (Washington, 1877.)]

[Footnote 2: That these assertions are not merely my own, but those of the most profound students of these tongues, will be seen from the following extracts, which could easily be added to:—

"This language [the Cree] will be found to be adequate, not only to the mere expression of their wants, but to that of every circumstance or sentiment that can, in any way, interest or affect uncultivated minds."—Joseph Howse, *A Grammar of the Cree Language*, p. 12. (London, 1865.)

"J'ai affirme que nos deux grandes langues du Nouveau Monde [the Iroquois and the Algonkin] etaient tres claires, tres precises, exprimant avec facilite non seulement les relations exterieures des idees, mais encore leur relations metaphysiques. C'est ce qu' out commence de demontrer mes premiers chapitres de grammaire, et ce qu'achevera de faire voir ce que je vais dire sur les verbes."—Rev. M. Cuoq, *Jugement Errone de M. Ernest Renan sur les Langues Sauvages.* p. 32 (2d Ed. Montreal, 1869.)

"Affermo che non e facile di trovare una lingua piu atta della Messicana a trattar le materie metafisiche; poiche e difficile di trovarne un' altra, che tanto abbondi, quanto quella, di nomi astratte."—Clavigero, *Storia Antica del Messico*, Tomo IV, p. 244. (Cesena, 1781.)

"Todos los bellisimos sentimientos que se albergan en los nobles corazones en ninguna otra de aquellas lenguas (Europeas) pueden encontrar una expresion tan viva tan patetica y energica como la que tienen en Mexicano. ?En cual otra se habla con tanto acatamiento, con veneracion tan profunda, de los altisimos mysterios de ineffable amor que nos muestra el Cristianismo?"—Fr. Agustin de la Rosa, in the *Eco de la Fe*. (Merida, 1870.)

Alcide d'Orbigny argues forcibly to the same effect, of the South American languages:—"Les Quichuas et les Aymaras civilises ont une langue etendue, pleine de figures elegantes, de comparaisons naives, de poesie, surtout lorsqu'il s'agit d'amour; et il ne faut pas croire qu'isoles au sein des forets sauvages ou jetes au milieu des plaines sans bornes, les peuples chasseurs, agriculteurs et guerriers, soient prives de formes elegantes, de figures riches et variees."—*L'Homme Americain*, Tome I, p. 154.

For other evidence see Brinton, *American Hero Myths*, p. 25. (Philadelphia, 1882.). Horatio Hale, *The Iroquois Book of Rites*, p. 107. (Philadelphia, 1883.)]

[Footnote 3: *Ethnography and Philology of the Hidatsa Indians*, p. 18.]

[Footnote 4: *The Tribes of California*, p. 73. (Washington, 1877.)]

[Footnote 5: "Il n'est pas rare de trouver des individus parlant jusqu'a trois ou quatre langues, aussi distinctes entr'elles que le francais et l'allemand."—Alcide D'Orbigny, *L'Homme Americain*, Tome I, p. 170. The generality of this fact in South America was noted by Humboldt, *Voyage aux Regions Tropicales*, T. III, p. 308.]

[Footnote 6: "Hay muchos de ellos buenos gramaticos, y componen oraciones largas y bien autorizadas, y versos exametros y pentametros."— Toribio de Motilinia, *Historia de los Indios de la Nueva Espana*, Tratado III, cap. XII.]

[Footnote 7: *Menologio Franciscano de los Varones mas Senalados de la Provincia de Mexico*, Tomo IV, pp. 447-9. (Mexico, 1871.)

In the Prologue to the *Sermonario Mexicano* of F. Juan de Bautista (Mexico, 1606), is a well-written letter, in Latin, by Don Antonio Valeriano, a native of Atzcaputzalco, who was professor of grammar and rhetoric in the College of Tlatilulco. Bautista says of him that he spoke extempore in Latin with the eloquence of a Cicero or a Quintilian; and his contemporary, the academician Francisco Cervantes Salazar, writes: "Magistrum habent [Indi] ejusdem nationis, Antonium Valerianum, nostris grammaticis nequaquam inferiorem, in legis christianae observatione satis doctum et ad eloquentiam avidissimum."—*Tres Dialogos Latinos de Francisco Cervantes Salazar*, p. 150 (Ed. Icazbalceta, Mexico, 1875).]

[Footnote 8: Francisco de Paula Garcia Pelaez, *Memorias para la Historia del Antiguo Reyno de Guatemala*, Tomo III, pp. 201 and 221 (Guatemala, 1852).]

[Footnote 9: *Ritos Antiguos, Sacrificios e Idolatrias de los Indios de la Nueva Espana*, in the *Coleccion de Documentos Ineditos para la Historia de Espana*, Tom. 53, p. 300.]

[Footnote 10: *A Study of the Manuscript Troano*. By Cyrus Thomas, Ph.D., with an Introduction by D.G. Brinton, M.D., p. xxvii. (Washington, 1883.)]

[Footnote 11: "Tenian libros de pergaminos que hacian de los cueros de venados, tan anchos como una mano o mas, e tan luengos como diez o doce passos, e mas e menos, que se encogian e doblaban e resumian en el tamano e grandeza de una mano por sus dobleces uno contra otro (a manera de reclamo); y en aquestos tenian pintados sus caracteres o figuras de tinta roxa o negra, de tal manera que aunque no eran letura ni escritura, significaban y se entendian por ellas todo lo que querian muy claramente."—Oviedo, *Historia General y Natural de Indias*, Lib. XLII, cap. I.]

[Footnote 12: "Une ecriture consistant en raies tracees sur de petites planchettes."—Alcide D'Orbigny, *L'Homme Americain*, Tomo L, p. 170, on the authority of Viedma, *Informe general de la Provincia de Santa Cruz, MS.*]

[Footnote 13: *Legends and Tales of the Eskimo*. (Edinburgh and London, 1875.)]

[Footnote 14: *Pok, Kalalek avalangnek, etc.*, Nongme, 1857; or, *Pok, en Groenlaender, som har reist og ved sin Hjemkomst, etc. Efter gamle Handskrifter fundne hos Groenlaendere ved Godthaab.* Godthaab, 1857.]

[Footnote 15: *Kaladlit Assilialit, etc.* See Thomas W. Field, *Indian Bibliography*, p. 199. (New York, 1873.)]

[Footnote 16: First printed in *The American Whig Review*, New York, Feb. 1849; reprinted in *The Indian Miscellany*, edited by W.W. Beach, Albany, 1877. I have not been able to find the original.]

[Footnote 17: Horatio Hale, *The Iroquois Book of Rites*. (Philadelphia, 1883.) It is No. II of my "Library of Aboriginal American Literature."

The introductory essay, in ten chapters, treats at considerable length of the ethnology and history of the Huron-Iroquois nations, the Iroquois League and its founders (Hiawatha, Dekanawidah, and their associates), the origin of the Book of Rites, the composition of the Federal Council, the clan system, the laws of the League, and the historical traditions relating to it, the Iroquois character and public policy, and the Iroquois language. A map prefixed to the work shows the location of the United Nations and of the surrounding tribes.]

[Footnote 18: *Recit de Francois Kaondinoketc, Chef des Nipissingues (tribu de race Algonquine) ecrit par lui-meme en 1848. — Traduit en Francais et accompagne de notes par* M.N.O., 8vo. pp. 8. (Paris, 1877.)]

[Footnote 19: *The National Legend of the Chata-Muskokee Tribes.* By Daniel G. Brinton, M.D. Morrisania, N.Y., 1870. 4to. pp. 13. Reprinted from *The Historical Magazine*, February, 1870.]

[Footnote 20: "Les chefs des vieillards m'avoient souvent parle de leurs ancetres, des courses qu'ils avoient faites, et des combats qu'ils avoient eu a soutenir, avant que la nation put se fixer ou elle est aujourd'hui. L'histoire de ces premiers Creeks, qui portoient alors le nom de Moskoquis, etoit conservee par des banderoles ou chapelets," etc. — *Memoire ou Coup-d'Oeil Rapide sur mes different Voyages et mon Sejour dans la Nation Creck*, Par le Gen. Milfort, pp. 48, 229. (Paris, An. XI, 1802).]

[Footnote 21: "We burned all we could find of them," writes Bishop Landa, "which pained the natives to an extraordinary degree." — *Relacion de las Cosas de Yucatan*, p. 316. For a discussion of what was destroyed at Mani see Cogolludo, *Historia de Yucatan*, 3d Ed., Vol. I, p. 604, note by the Editor. The efforts which have of late been made by Senor Icazbalceta and the Reverend Canon Carrillo to modify the general opinion of these acts of vandalism cannot possibly be successful. The ruthless hostility of the Church to the ancient civilization, an hostility founded on religious intolerance, could be proved by hundreds of extracts from the early writers.]

[Footnote 22: Boturini's work is entitled *Idea de una Nueva Historia General de la America Septentrional fundada sobre material copioso defiguras, Symbolos, Caracteres, y Geroglificos, Cantares y Manuscritos de Autores Indios.* Madrid, 1746. The fate of his collection is sketched by Brasseur de Bourbourg, in the introduction to his *Histoire des Nations civilisees de Mexique et de l'Amerique Centrale*, Vol I.]

[Footnote 23: The following extract from Ixtlilxochitl sums up the native authorities on which he relied for the particulars of the life of the last prince of Tezcuco, and merits quotation as a bit of literary history: —

"Autores son de todo lo referido, y de los demas de su vida y hechos los infantes de Mexico Ytzcoatzin y Xiuhcozcatzin, y otros Poetas y Historicos en los anales de las tres cabezas de esta Nueva Espana, y en particular en los anales que hizo el infante Quauhtlazaciulotzin, primer Senor del pueblo de Chiauhtla; y asimismo se halla en las relaciones que escribieron los infantes de la ciudad de Tezcuco, Don Pablo, Don Toribio, Don Hernando Pimentel y Juan de Pomar hijos y nietos del Rey Nezalhualpiltzintli de Tezcuco, y asimismo el infante Don Alonso Axiaicatzin Senor de Itztapalapan, hijo del rey de Cuitlahuac, y sobrino del rey Motecutzomatzin." —Ixtlilxochitl, *Historia Chichimeca*, cap. XLIX.]

[Footnote 24: In the celebrated library of J.F. Ramirez, were two folio volumes, containing 1022 pages, entitled *Anales Antiguos de Mexico y sus Contornos*. They included, besides various Spanish accounts, 27 fragments in the Nahuatl language, some translated and some not. The titles of all are given by Don Joaquin Garcia Icazbalceta, in his valuable and rare *Apuntes para un Catalogo de Escritores en Lenguas Indigenas de America*, pp. 140-142. (Mexico, 1866.)]

[Footnote 25: *Memorial del Pueblo de Teptlaustuque, en la Nueva Espana; en que se refiere su Origen i Poblacion, i de los Tributos i Servicios, antes i despues de la Conquista; todo pintado, i M.S.* En la Libreria del Rei. Antonio de Leon i Pinelo, *Bibliotheca Occidental*. The district of Tepetlaoztoc belonged to Tezcuco.]

[Footnote 26: "Don Gabriel Castaneda, Indio principal, natural de Michuacan Colomocho en la Provincia de Mejico. Escribio en Lengua Megicana, *Relacion* de la Jornada que hizo Sandoval Acaxitli, Cacique y Senor de Tlalmanalco, con el Sr. Visorey Don Antonio de Mendoza en la Conquista de los Chichimecas de Xuchipila, 1541." —Beristain y Souza, *Biblioteca Hispano-Americana Septentrional*, s.v.]

[Footnote 27: For testimony to this interesting fact see *The Maya Chronicles*, Introduction, p. 28, note.]

[Footnote 28: *The Books of Chilan Balam, The Prophetic and Historic Records of the Mayas of Yucatan.* By Daniel G. Brinton, M.D., Philadelphia, 1882. Reprint from the *Penn Monthly*, March, 1882.]

[Footnote 29: *Library of Aboriginal American Literature*, Vol. I, p. 189. (Philadelphia, 1882.)]

[Footnote 30: An intelligent appreciation of the linguistic labors of Pio Perez was written by Dr. Berendt, in 1871, and printed in Mexico.—*Los Trabajos Linguisticos de Don Juan Pio Perez.* 8vo. pp. 6.]

[Footnote 31: *Disertacion sobre la Historia de la Lengua Maya o Yucateca*. Por Crescencio Carrillo. Published in the *Revista de Merida*, 1870.]

[Footnote 32: A fine manuscript of Vico's work, as well as a number of other productions in Cakchiquel, by the missionaries, are in the library of the American Philosophical Society, at Philadelphia.]

[Footnote 33: Tecpan Atitlan is a village on the shore of Lake Atitlan, in the province of Solola, Guatemala.]

[Footnote 34: Don Domingo Juarros, *Compendio de la Historia de la Ciudad de Guatemala*, Tomo, II pp. 6, 7, 12, 16, et al. (Ed. Guatemala, 1857). A copy of Tzumpan's writings is said to be in a private library in the United States.

The native Cakchiquel writers were also the authorities on which Father Vazquez depended, in part, in composing his history of Guatemala. He gives a partial translation of one, beginning the passage: "Los Indios de Zolola dizen en sus escritos," etc.—Fray Francisco Vazquez, *Cronica de la Provincia de Guatemala*, Lib. III, Cap. XXXVI. (Guatemala, 1714, 1716.)]

[Footnote 35: Brasseur de Bourbourg, *Bibliotheque Mexico-Guatemalienne*, p. 142. (Paris, 1871.)]

[Footnote 36: *Titulos de la Casa de Ixcuin-Nehaib, Senora del Territorio de Otzoya*. Guatemala, 1876. 8vo. pp. 15. Reprint from the *Boletin de la Sociedad Economica de Guatemala*.]

[Footnote 37: *Las Historias del Origen de los Indios de esta Provincia de Guatemala, traducidas de la lengua Quiche al Castellano*. Por el R.P.F. Francisco Ximenez. 8vo. Vienna, 1857.]

[Footnote 38: *Popol Vuh. Le Livre Sacre et les Mythes de l'Antiquite Americaine, avec les livres heroiques et historiques des Quiches*. Par l'Abbe Brasseur de Bourbourg. (Paris, 1861.)]

[Footnote 39: *The Names of the Gods in the Kiche Myths of Central America*. By Daniel G. Brinton, M.D. 8vo. pp. 37. (Philadelphia, 1881.) Reprint from the *Proceedings* of the American Philosophical Society, 1881.]

[Footnote 40: Boturini, *Idea de una Nueva Historia de la America Septentrional*, p. 115.]

[Footnote 41: Cabrera, *Teatro Critico Americano*, p 33.]

[Footnote 42: *American Hero-Myths*, pp. 213-217. (Philadelphia, 1882.)]

[Footnote 43: On this Qquichua MS. see Marcos Jimenez de la Espada, *Tres Relaciones de Antiguedades Peruanas*. Introd. p. 34.]

[Footnote 44: *Relacion de las Costumbres Antiguas de los Naturales del Piru*, printed in the work last quoted, p. 142, note.]

[Footnote 45: "En cabildo de 29 de Julio de 1692, el capitan Don Antonio de Fuentes y Guzman trajo a esta sala siete peticiones escritas en cortezas de arboles." — Francisco de Paula Garcia Pelaez, *Memorias para la Historia del Antiguo Reyno de Guatemala*, Tom. II, p. 267. (Guatemala, 1852.)]

[Footnote 46: *O Selvagem. Trabalho Preparatorio para aproveitamento de Selvagem e de solo por elle occupado no Brazil*. Rio de Janeiro, 1876.]

[Footnote 47: *Notes on the Lingoa Geral, or Modern Tupi of the Amazonas*, in the *Transactions* of the American Philological Association, for 1872.]

[Footnote 48: Boturini, *Idea de una Nueva Historia*, etc., App. pp. 57 et seq.; Didacus Valades, *Rhetorica Christiana*, Pars Secunda (Perusia, 1579); Gemelli Carreri, *Giro del Mundo*.]

[Footnote 49: Stephens, *Travels in Yucatan*, Vol. I, p. 449 (London, 1843).]

[Footnote 50: *Relacion de las Ceremonias y Ritos de Mechoacan*. The MS. of this work, in the Library of Congress, does not contain the Calendar which the author, in the body of the work, promises to append; nor apparently does the copy in Madrid, from which the work was printed, in Vol. 53 of the *Coleccion de Documentos Ineditos para la Historia de Espana*.]

[Footnote 51: *Pintura del Gobernador, Alcaldes y Regidores de Mexico. Codex en Geroglificos Mexicanos y en lengua Castellana y Azteca.* First published at Madrid, 1878. A specimen of the map, "Carte Geographique Azteque," is given by Professor Leon de Rosny, in *Les Documents Ecrit de l'Antiquite Americaine*, p. 70 (Paris, 1882).]

[Footnote 52: Stephens, *Travels in Yucatan*, Vol. II, p. 265, gives a Maya map of Mani. A more complete study of the subject is that of Carrillo, *Geografia Maya*, in the *Anales del Museo Nacional de Mexico*, Tom. II, p. 435.]

[Footnote 53: *Silabario de Idioma Mexicano, dispuesto por el* Lic. Faustino Chimalpopocatl Galicia, Mexico, 1849, 8vo. pp. 16. Second edition, Mexico, 1859, 8vo. pp. 32. Also *Epitome o Modo Facil de Aprender el Idioma Nahuatl*, 12mo. pp. 124, Mexico, 1869.]

[Footnote 54: *Elementos de la Gramatica Megicana*, por Don Antonio Tobar Cano y Moctezuma. Written about 1642.]

[Footnote 55: *Confessionario Mayor y Menor en Lengua Mexicana, y Platicas contra las Supersticiones de Idolatria, que el dia de oy an quedado a los Naturales desta Nueva Espana.* Ano de 1634. Mexico. A copy of this scarce volume is in my library.]

[Footnote 56: Dr. Couto de Magalhaes remarks: "Como o nome indica, este missionario devia ser algum mestico que, com o leite materno, beben os primeiros rudimentos da grande lingua Sul-Americana." —*Origens, Costumes e Regias Selvagem*, p. 62 (Rio de Janeiro, 1876). In 1876 M. Varuhagen published, at Vienna, a *Historia da paixao de Christo e taboa dos parentescos em lingua Tupi*, written by Yapuguay, an extract, apparently, from the volume mentioned in the text. The edition was only 100 copies.]

[Footnote 57: C.F. Hartt, *On the Lingoa Geral of the Amazonas*, p. 3, in the *Transactions* of the American Philological Association, 1872.]

[Footnote 58: *Tah-gah-jute; or, Logan and Cresap. An Historical Essay.* By Brantz Mayer. (Albany, 1867.)]

[Footnote 59: *History of the American Indians*, pp. 52, 63. (London, 1775.)]

[Footnote 60: James Howse, A Grammar of the Cree Language, p. 11. (London, 1865.)]

[Footnote 61: "Piensan que un hombre que habla sin cortarse y con soltura debe ser de una naturaleza superior y privilegiada. Por solo esta circumstancia ascienden el grado de Ghulmenes o caciques, u hombres notables." Federico Barbara, *Manual o Vocabulario de la Lengua Pampa*, p. 164. (Buenos Aires, 1879.)]

[Footnote 62: Rev. Cyrus Byington, *Grammar of the Choctaw Language*, p. 20 (Philadelphia, 1870.)]

[Footnote 63: *Huehue*, ancient; *tlatolli*, words, speeches. A special variety were the *calmecatlatolli*, the declamations which the youths of noble families were taught to deliver in the spacious halls of the *calmecac*, or public schools. "Calmeca tlatolli, palabras dichas en corredores largos. E tomase por los dichos y fictiones de los viejos antiguos." Molina, *Vocabulario de la Lengua Mexicana, sub voce*. The word *calmecac* is a compound of *calli*, house, and *mecana*, to give, it being the building furnished by the State for purposes of public instruction.]

[Footnote 64: Fr. Juan Baptista (or Bautista), *Platicas Morales en Lengua Mexicana, intitulados Huehuetlatolli*, 8vo. Mexico (1599? or 1601?). This work is not mentioned by Icazbalceta, but is described in Berendt's notes, and a copy was sold in Paris in 1869. It is enumerated by Vetancurt, *Menologio Franciscano*, p. 446 (2d ed.).]

[Footnote 65: Olmos, *Grammaire de la Langue Nahuatl*, pp. 231 sqq. (Paris 1875.)]

[Footnote 66: *Narratives of the Rites and Laws of the Incas.* Translated by C. R. Markham. Printed for the Hackluyt Society (London, 1873).]

[Footnote 67: *Chrestomathie de la Langue Maya*, in *Etude sur le Systeme Graphique et la Langue des Mayas.* (Paris, 1870.)]

[Footnote 68: Bernal Diaz gives an interesting account of this "black sermon," as he calls it. The incident is significant, as it shows that the natives were accustomed to gather around their places of worship, to listen to addresses by the priests. See the *Historia Verdadera de la Conquista de la Nueva Espana*, Cap. XXVII. (Madrid, 1632.)]

[Footnote 69: Some judicious remarks on the origin and development of aboriginal poetry are offered by Theodore Baker, in his excellent monograph on the music of the North American Indians, but his field of view was somewhat too restricted to do the subject full justice, as, indeed, he acknowledges. *Über die Musik der Nord-Americanischen Wilden*, von Theodor Baker, pp. 6-14. (Leipzig, 1882.)]

[Footnote 70: Schoolcraft, *History, Condition and Prospects of the Indian Tribes of the United States*, vol. V, p. 559.]

[Footnote 71: *Grammaire et Vocabulaire de la Langue Taensa, avec Textes traduits et commentes.* Par J.D. Haumonte, Parisot, et L. Adam. Paris, 1882.]

[Footnote 72: "Or, i'ay assez de commerce avec la poesie pour juger cecy, que non seulement il n'y a rien de barbaric en cette imagination, mais qu'elle est tout a faict anacreontique."—*Essais de Michel de Montaigne*, Liv. I, cap. XXX, and comp. cap. XXXVI.]

[Footnote 73: "Chez les Guarayos, ces hymnes religieux et allegoriques, si riches en figures.—Il est impossible de trouver rien de plus gracieux."

"Quant a leurs poetes, le charme avec lequel ils peignent l'amour, annonce, certainement en eux, une intelligence developpee et autant d'esprit que de sensibilite."—Alcide D'Orbigny, *L'Homme Americain*, Tome I, pp. 155, 170.]

[Footnote 74: "Negli avanci, che si restano della lor Poesia, vi sono alcuni versi, ne'quali tra le parole significative si vedono frapposte certe interjezioni, o sillabe prive d'ogni significazione, e soltanto adoperate, per quel ch'appare, per aggiustarsi al metro. Il linguaggio della lor Poesia era puro, ameno, brilliante, figurato, e fregiato di frequenti comparazioni fatte colle cose piu piacevoli della natura, siccome fiori, alberi, ruscelli, &c." — *Clavigero, Storia di Messico*. Tom. II, p. 175.]

[Footnote 75: The originals of some of these poems were in the hands of Ixtlilxochitl, as is evident from his *Historia Chichimeca*, cap. XLVII.]

[Footnote 76: Sahagun, *Psalmodia Xpiana*. (Mexico, 1583?) An extremely rare book, which I have never seen. Clavigero saw a copy, and thinks it was printed about 1540. *Storia di Messico*, Tom. II, p, 178, Note.]

[Footnote 77: It is mentioned by Icazbalceta, *Apuntes para un Catalogo de Escritores en Lenguas Indigenas de America*, p. 146. (Mexico, 1866.) There are, however, two copies of it extant, somewhere.]

[Footnote 78: See Mr. Clements R. Markham's Introductions to his edition of the *Ollanta* drama (London, 1871); and to his *Qquichua Grammar and Dictionary* (London, 1864).]

[Footnote 79: "I'en demeurai tout rauy; mais aussi toutes les fois qu'il m'en ressouuient, le coeur m'en tressaillant, il me semble que ie les aye encor aux oreilles." — Jean de Lery, *Histoire d'un voyage faict en la terre du Bresil, autrement dite Amerique*, pp. 258, 286. (Geneve, 1585.)]

[Footnote 80: See his *Origens, Costumes e Regiaeo Selvagem*, pp. 78-82, 140-147. (Rio de Janeiro, 1876.)]

[Footnote 81: Spix and Martius, *Reise in Brasilien, Brasilianische Volkslieder und Indianische Melodien, Musikbeilage*.]

[Footnote 82: *Une Fete Bresilienne celebree a Rouen en 1550 suivie d'un Fragment du XVI'e Siecle roulant sur la Theogonie des anciens Peuples du Bresil et des Poesies en Langue Tupique, de Christovam Valente*. Par Ferdinand Denis, pp. 36-51, 98, sqq. (Paris, 1850.)]

[Footnote 83: The Arawack language, which is now spoken in Guiana only, at the time of the discovery extended over the Greater and Lesser Antilles and the Bahama Islands, as I have shown in an essay on *The Arawack Language of Guiana in its Linguistic and Ethnological Relations*, in the *Transactions* of the American Philosophical Society, 1870.]

[Footnote 84: *The Memoirs of Lieutenant Henry Timberlake*, p. 80 (London 1765).]

[Footnote 85: In the ancient Qquichua literature the tragic dramas were called *huancay*; those of a comic nature, *aranhuay*. Both were composed in assonant verses of six and eight syllables, which were not sung or chanted, but repeated with dramatic intonation.]

[Footnote 86: On the bibliography of the drama see Zegarra, *Ollantai, Drame en Vers Quechuas du temps des Incas*, Introd. p. CLXXIII. (Paris, 1878.) The English translation is by Clements R. Markham, *Ollanta, an Ancient Ynca Drama* (London, 1871).]

[Footnote 87: The recent attempt of General Don Bartolome Mitre, of Buenos Ayres, to discredit the antiquity of the Ollanta drama (in the *Nueva Revista de Buenos Ayres*, 1881), has been most thoroughly and conclusively refuted by Mr. Clements R. Markham, in the volume of the Hackluyt Society's Publications for 1883.]

[Footnote 88: *Rabinal-Achi, ou le Drame Ballet du Tun*, published as an appendix to the *Grammaire de la Langue Quiche* (Paris, 1862). The Abbe Brasseur asserts that he wrote down this drama from verbal information, at the village of Rabinal in Guatemala; but a note by Dr. Berendt in my possession characterizes this statement as incorrect, and adds: "Brasseur found the MS. all written, in the hands of an hacendado, on the road from Guatemala to Chiapas. The original exists still in the same place." It was a weakness with the Abbe to throw, designedly, considerable obscurity about his authorities and the sources of his knowledge.]

* * * * *

INDEX

Mendoza, Ant., de
Mendoza, G.
Mexicans
Michoacan
Milfort, Gen.
Mitre, B.
Molina, A.
Montaigne, M.
Motolinia, T. de
Moxos
Muskokees
Muyscas

Nahuatl Language Nahuatl-Spanish Dialect *Nakuk Pech Nehaib, Titles of Nezahualcoyotl Nezahualpilli* Nicaraguans Nipissings Nunez de la Vega.

Ojibways *Ollanta, The Ollita, The* Olmos, Andre de Omahas Oviedo, F.

Pachacuti, Don J. Pampas, Tribes of *Pasiones, Las* Pelaez, F.P. Garcia Pequods Perez, Juan Pio Peruvians *Pimentel, Ant. Pimentel, H.* Pipils Pocomans *Pok* Ponce, Pedro *Pomar, J. de Popol Vuh, The* Powers, S. *Prophecies of Mayas*

Queh, F.T.G.
Quiches, see *Kiches*
Qquichuas
Quipus

Rabinal Achi Rafinesque, C.S. Ramirez, J.F. Rink, Dr. H. *Rosa, A. de la* Rosny, Leon de

Sahagun, B. de
Salazar, F.C.
San Antonio, J. de
Sanchez Solis, F.
Scherzer, C.
Schoolcraft, H.R.
Sequoyah
Simeon, Remi
Sioux
Six Nations
Smith, B.
Solola, Province
Squier, E.G.

Taensas *Tanner, J.* Tarascos *Tecpan Atitlan* Tezcuco *Tezozomoc, F. de A.* Theologia Indorum Thomas, C. Timberlake, H. Timucuana Tlatilulco, College of *Tlaxcallan, History of Tobar, Ant.* Tomar, *J.B. de Tonalamatl, The* Torres, *J.* Tupis Tuscaroras *Tzolante, The* Tzendals *Tzumpan, F.G.C.*

Valades, D.
Valeriano, Antonio
Varnhagen, M.
Vazquez, F.
Vetancurt, A. de
Vico, Domingo de
Viracocha
Votan

Walum Olum Ward, Dr. Wyandotts

Xahila, F.E.A. Ximenez, F.

Zacicoxol, the Zapata y Mendoza, J.V. Zapotecs Zegarra, G.P. Zoque language Zunis

* * * * *

Library of Aboriginal American Literature.

General Editor and Publisher, DANIEL G. BRINTON, M.D.,

115 South Seventh St., Philadelphia, Pa., United States.

The European Market will be supplied by

NICHOLAS TRÜBNER & CO., 57 & 59 Ludgate Hill, London, England.

The aim of this series is to put within the reach of scholars authentic materials for the study of the languages, history and culture of the native races of North and South America. Each of the works selected will be the production of a native author, and will be printed in the original tongue, with an English translation and notes. Most of them will be from unpublished manuscripts, and they will form a series indispensable to the future student of American archaeology, ethnology or linguistics. They will be printed FROM TYPE, AND IN LIMITED EDITIONS ONLY. The volumes will be sold SEPARATELY, at moderate prices, either in paper or bound in cloth. They will all be planted on heavy laid paper, of the best quality. The following have already appeared: —

* * * * *

NO. I. THE MAYA CHRONICLES.

Edited by DANIEL G. BRINTON, M.D.

1 vol., 8vo, pp. 279. Price, paper, $3.00; cloth, $3.50.

This volume contains five brief chronicles in the Maya language of Yucatan, written shortly after the Conquest, and carrying the history of that people back many centuries. To these is added a history of the Conquest, written in his native tongue, by a Maya Chief, in 1562. The texts are preceded by an introduction on the history of the Mayas; their language, calendar, numeral system, etc.; and a vocabulary is added at the close.

NOTICES OF THE PRESS.

"We hope that Dr. Brinton will receive every encouragement in his labors to disclose to Americans these literary antiquities of the Continent. He eminently deserves it, both by the character of his undertaking and the quality of his work." — *The American* (Phila.)

"It would be difficult to praise too highly the task Dr. Brinton has set before him. Prepared by long studies in the same field, he does not undertake the work as a novice. ... There should be no hesitation among those who wish well to American antiquarianism in subscribing to the series edited and published by Dr. Brinton." — *The Critic.*

"Dr. Brinton's work upon the history of the Mayas or Aborigines of Yucatan [the "Maya Chronicles"] is a most important contribution to the literature of American antiquities. ... Comparative linguists, as well as archaeologists, will find a new and very interesting subject of study in these remains." — *The Saturday Review* (London).

"The efforts of Dr. Brinton will be welcomed by all antiquarian students, for they are not only original contributions, but are also presented in a readable and interesting manner." — *The American Antiquarian.*

* * * * *

No. II. The IROQUOIS BOOK OF RITES.

Edited by HORATIO HALE, Esq.

1 vol., 8vo. Price, paper, $3.00; cloth, $3.50.

The "BOOK OF RITES" is a native composition, which was preserved orally for centuries, and was written down about a century ago. It gives the speeches, songs and ceremonies which were rehearsed when a chief died and his successor was appointed. The fundamental laws of the League, a list of their ancient towns, and the names of the chiefs who composed their first council, are also comprised in the work. It may be said to carry the authentic history of Northern America back to a period fifty years earlier than the era of Columbus. The introductory essay treats of the ethnology and history of the Huron-Iroquois League and its founders, the origin of the Book of Rites, the composition of the Federal Council, the clan system, the laws of the League, and the Iroquois character, public policy, and language.

NOTICES OF THE PRESS AND OF EMINENT WRITERS.

"This work may be said to open a field of Indian research new to ethnologists. ... These precious relics of antiquity are concise in their wording, and full of meaning. ... The additions made by Mr. Hall are almost as valuable as the texts themselves." — *The Nation* New York, September 13, 1883.

"The reputation of the author, added to this fascinating title, will insure its favorable reception, not only by ethnologists, but also, the reading public. ... A remarkable discovery, and indisputably of great ethnological value. ... A book which is as suggestive as this must bear good fruit." — *Science*, August 31,1883.

"The work contains much new material of permanent interest and value to the historical scholar and the scientist. ... " — *The Magazine of American History*, September, 1883.

"In this Book of Rites we have poetry, law, history, tradition and genealogy, interesting and valuable for many reasons...." — *Good Literature*, August 18, 1883.

"The Book of Rites is edited by the eminent philologist, Mr. Horatio Hale, who has done so much to elucidate the whole subject of Indian ethnography and migrations, with the argument derived from language in connection with established tradition; and especially to disentangle Iroquois history from its complications with the legends of their mythology." — *Auburn Daily Advertiser*, July 21, 1883.

"The book is one of great ethnological value, in the light it casts on the political and social life, as well as the character and capacity, of the people with whom it originated." — *Popular Science Monthly*, November 1883.

"It is a philosophical and masterly treatise on the Iroquois league and the cognate tribes, their relations, language, mental characteristics and polity, such as we have never had of any nation of this Continent...." — *Dr. J. Gilmary Shea.*

"It is full of instructive hints, particularly as bearing on the state of so-called savages before they are brought in contact with so-called civilized men. Such evidence is, from the nature of the case, very difficult to obtain, and therefore all the more valuable...." —*Prof. F. Max Mueller.*

"It gives us a much clearer insight into the formation and workings of the Iroquois league than we before possessed." —*Hon. George S. Conover.*

"It contains more that is authentic and new, of the Iroquois nations, than any other single work with which I am acquainted." —*Rev. Charles Hawley, D.D.*

* * * * *

No. III. THE COMEDY-BALLET OF GÜEGÜENCE.

Edited by DANIEL G. BRINTON, M.D.

1 vol., 8vo. Paper, $2.00; Cloth, $2.50.

A curious and unique specimen of the native comic dances, with dialogues, called *bailes*, formerly common in Central America. It is in the mixed Nahuatl-Spanish jargon of Nicaragua, and shows distinctive features of native authorship. The Introduction treats of the ethnology of Nicaragua, and the local dialects, musical instruments, and dramatic representations of that section of our continent. A map and a number of illustrations are added.

Other important works, in various native languages, are in the course of preparation, under competent editorship.

Of these may be mentioned—

THE NATIONAL LEGEND OF THE CREEKS. Edited by A.S. GATSCHET.

The original account, written in 1735; an English translation, and a re-translation into the Creek language, in which it was originally delivered, by an educated native, and into the Hitchiti, a dialect cognate to the Creek.

THE ANNALS OF THE KAKCHIQUELS. By ERNANTEZ XAHILA.

These chronicles are the celebrated *Memorial de Tecpan Atitlan* so often quoted by the late Abbe Brasseur de Bourbourg. They are invaluable for the ancient history and mythology of Gautemalan nations, and are of undoubted authenticity and antiquity.

THE ANNALS OF QUAUHTITLAN. Edited by A.F. BANDELIER.

The original Aztec text, with a new translation. This is also known as the *Codex Chimalpopoca*. It is one of the most curious and valuable documents in Mexican archaeology.

ABORIGINAL AMERICAN ANTHOLOGY. Edited by DANIEL G. BRINTON, M.D.

A collection of the songs, chants and metrical compositions of the Indians, designed to display the emotional and imaginative powers of the race and the prosody of their languages.

* * * * *

The following two works are not portions of the series, but are related to it by their contents. They may be obtained from the same publishers.

AMERICAN HERO-MYTHS.

A STUDY in the NATIVE RELIGIONS of the WESTERN CONTINENT.

By DANIEL G. BRINTON, A.M., M.D., etc.

1 vol., 8vo, pp. 251. (Philad'a, 1882.) Cloth, Price, $1.75.

NOTICES OF THE PRESS.

"Dr. Brinton writes from a minute and extended knowledge of the original sources. ... His work renders a signal service to the cause of comparative mythology in our country." — *The Literary World* (Boston).

"This study of certain of the most remarkable stories of American mythology is exceedingly interesting." — *The Saturday Review* (London).

"In his 'American Hero-Myths' Dr. Brinton gives us the clue to the religious thought of the aboriginal Races. ... It is a learned and careful book, clearly written, popular in style though scientific in method, and must be a good deal fresher than a novel to most readers." — *The American* (Philadelphia).

"This volume is the first attempt at what is entitled to be regarded as a critically accurate presentation of the fundamental conceptions found in the native beliefs of the tribes of America." — *The New England Bibliopolist.*

"This is a thoughtful and original contribution to the science of comparative religion." — *The Boston Journal.*

"We regard the 'Hero Myths' as a valuable contribution to the history of religion and to comparative mythology." — *The Teacher* (Philadelphia).

"...These few extracts give no idea of the mass of legends in this volume, and the queer, out-of-the-way information it supplies concerning the ideas and usages of races now extinct or hastening to extinction." — *The Dublin Evening Mail.*

"Dr. Brinton, in his 'American Hero-Myths,' has applied the comparative method soberly, and backed it by solid research in the original authors." — *The Critic* (New York).

ABORIGINAL AMERICAN AUTHORS, AND THEIR PRODUCTIONS.

Especially those in the Native Languages. A Contribution to the History of Literature.

By DANIEL G. BRINTON, A.M., M.D., etc.

1 vol., 8vo, pp. 63. Boards. Price, $1.00.

An essay founded on an address presented to the Congress of Americanists, at Copenhagen, in 1883. It is an extended review of the literary efforts of the red race, in their own tongues, and in English, Latin and Spanish (both manuscript and printed). An entirely novel field of inquiry is opened to view, of equal interest to ethnologists, linguists and historians.

End of Project Gutenberg's Aboriginal American Authors, by Daniel G. Brinton